The Sun Always Shines for the Cool
A Midnight Moon at the Greasy Spoon
Eulogy for a Small Time Thief

by

Miguel Piñero

Arte Publico Press
Houston, 1984

ACKNOWLEDGEMENTS

Sincere thanks to the Guggenheim Foundation for the fellowship which made the preparation of this volume possible.

Miguel Piñero

Books by Miguel Piñero:
Short Eyes
The Bodega Sold Dreams

Arte Público Press
Revista Chicano-Riqueña
University of Houston
University Park
Houston, Texas 77004

CONTENTS

The Sun Always Shines for the Cool

CHARACTERS

VIEJO

JUSTICE

CHILE GIRL

CAT EYES

PHEBE REED

WILLIE "B" BODEGA

KAHLU

JR. BALLOON

ROSA

DIAMOND RING

SATISFACTION

LEFTY "G" GORILLA

BAM-BAM BOY

A MAN

A PROSTITUTE

ACT I

Actors come in from hustling on the streets with the audience.
SETTING: A bar in a large city, the time is NOW . . . it's about midnight
and the place is preparing for business. This is a place for the hustlers and
players of the city. All the people are extremely well-dressed. There's soft
jazz coming out of the jukebox. There is a large sign over the bar:
"PUSHERS, IF YOU ARE BUSTED PUSHING IN HERE, YOU
WILL BE PUSHED INTO YOUR GRAVE."

ONSTAGE: Lefty at bar. Chile and Viva are running through a song at
piano. Phebe enters with two prostitutes.

PHEBE: With me it was in a pickup truck . . . I was hitching a
   runaway . . . where I was going I didn't know, but I was leaving
   where I was coming from . . .this guy pulls up and lets me in . . .
PROSTITUTE: Why was you running away from home?
PHEBE: It's a long story . . . one thing was my daddy. He was, well,
   hard to describe. He was a slob . . . a real slob . . . always fighting
   with my mother . . . and, well, once he found out that I screwed
   his brother . . . Actually it was the other way around. He screwed
   me 'cause I really didn't know what I was doing, being just eight
   years old. And my father instead of fucking up his brother, he
   took some money from him and kept quiet about the whole
   thing. I heard them in the living room . . . and my father was
   saying, well, she might as well learn to make money out of it.
   Like, one day the family went out to do some shopping and I
   stayed home. It was hot so I was taking a shower and he came
   into the bathroom and took off his clothes and jumped in the
   shower with me and he started telling me how he fed me, clothed
   me, housed me, the whole number. And then he did the same
   thing that his brother did and told me not to say anything to
   mom. I then knew that what he was doing was something that
   was not right. But as the years went by, he stayed away from me,
   but I just couldn't stand to be around him. So one day I just got
   what little things I had and split . . .
PROSTITUTE: You know, you sure take a long time to get where
   you're going.
PHEBE: Okay . . . Okay . . . well, this guy pulls over and tells me that
   he *knew* that I was a working girl and I thought that he meant
   that I had a job . . . then he asked me for a job . . . and I told him I

can't give you a job. I didn't owned anything for him . . . and he said, "Come on, woman, you understand what I mean. Maybe where you come from they have another name for it, but I want a blow job. . . ." So I start to blow air at him . . . then he said, "Oh, I see, money takes the action with you, huh? Okay . . .here." Pulls out ten dollars, hands it to me. Pulls out dick, shoves it in my mouth and when it over, he had to pull me away 'cause I didn't know when he wanted me to stop. He tells me that I work out good and what was my regular place of work. I told him I didn't have any and he took me to meet this woman who ran a bar. Well, from there on I just said to myself, "Well, this is one way of living and it's easy and I really get down to it. I kinda enjoy the work in a way. . . ." Well, a few years back I came up North and here I am . . .

CHILE: Boring.

LEFTY G.: Listen, get your back off the bar . . . you know better than giving your back to the bar.

PHEBE: You know something, Lefty, for an old motherfucker, you got a nerve to talk to me.

CHILE: Why not run the bar on the sap, Lefty? Teach her a lesson.

PHEBE: Why don't you mind your own business.

CHILE: Phebe, this is my business, and if you open up them painted bubble gum lips of yours again . . . I'll shove that blond wig down your throat, bitch.

PHEBE: Ohhh, go bitch, go on . . . come, that's right, just one step more.

LEFTY G.: Put that razor down, woman, or they'll be putting a tag on your big toe tonight . . . you hear me, woman?

JUSTICE: Hey. What the hell is going on here?

LEFTY G.: This bitch with the razor . . .

JUSTICE: Woman, put that thing away. . . . Lefty, I want you to count to ten, and if that thing ain't on the floor, I want you to put a hole in her head.

LEFTY G.: Right . . . seven . . . eight . . . nine . . .

PHEBE: Hold it . . . hold it. Okay, there. Justice, she ain't got no right calling me a sap.

LEFTY G.: Chile said I should run the bar on her.

CHILE: She was going to cut me with that razor.

JUSTICE: It's your stroke . . . stroke it. Kick her ass.

CHILE: Come, bitch. I'll whip your tight little ass like I own you . . . bitch . . . (*They begin to fight.*)

BAM-BAM: Mátala, Chile . . . mátala cabrona, mátala . . . Ooooh, pantaletas sucias . . . bien chingada.

JUSTICE: Okay, Chile girl, that's enough, you proved your point. . . . Bam-Bam, get your ass in the kitchen.

CHILE: Next time you pull a razor on me, I'll cut you from your throat to your trick filled pussy . . . bitch.

PHEBE: You called me a sap.

JUSTICE: That's just what you are . . . a sap. . . . You disrespect my place, and then you pull a razor on my girl, and you goddam well knew you wasn't going to use the damn thing . . . 'cuz you ain't ready to die.

PHEBE: Please, Justice, I'm sorry.

JUSTICE: Sorry, didn't do it . . . Phebe Reed did. Who's your man now?

PHEBE: Cat Eyes. (*Chile crosses to her.*)

JUSTICE: Cat Eyes, huh? . . . Run the bar on her.

LEFTY G.: Ain't nobody here, Justice, but Viejo.

JUSTICE: Viejo . . . where is he?

LEFTY G.: In the bathroom taking a shit.

JUSTICE: I don't need all the details, Lefty. Why didn't you tell me he was here?

LEFTY G.: I couldn't . . . not with that bitch giving us all this static.

JUSTICE: Run an hour on her.

PHEBE: Justice . . . please, Cat Eyes will kill me.

JUSTICE: He ain't gonna kill you, just touch you up a bit . . . the very thing you need too. Chile, tell Cat Eyes I wanna see him when he come in.

PHEBE: Please, Justice, give me some.

JUSTICE: Okay, you got some justice . . . next time. Hey, holy shitballs . . . Viejo, you fowl, stink-breath, low lifed, high-living son of a street walker, how the fuck you been?

VIEJO: Hey, toiletbowl mouth, long time no see, man.

PHEBE: Justice, this motherfucker eighty-sixed me.

JUSTICE: I already told you, you copped. Right? Now kindly vacate these premises and do not enter again through them doors, unless you are accompanied by your man or a john. Is that clear?

PHEBE: Thank you.

JUSTICE: Put an egg in your shoe and beat it!

VIEJO: Qué pasa with her?

JUSTICE: Violate número uno house rule.

VIEJO: Still the same rules, huh?

8

JUSTICE: Oh, fuck you . . . and get your back off the bar, you gray-ass, high-yellow, Puerto Rican nigger.

LEFTY G.: Want me to run the bar on him, Justice.

JUSTICE: You could if you wanna . . . but I think Chile girl will crack your skull for you if you do.

LEFTY G.: Blood is thicker than whiskey.

JUSTICE: Viejo, it's now been . . .

VIEJO: Five years, two weeks and three days.

JUSTICE: You been in, huh? I thought so.

VIEJO: How's things been going?

JUSTICE: Not bad. On Saturdays I make as much money from the undercovers—plainclothes and provacateurs—as I do from the players.

VIEJO: Tap?

JUSTICE: The whole joint.

VIEJO: Bad scene.

JUSTICE: It's them so-called revolutionary, loud-mouth militants . . . using places like these to make their meetings. Then the pushers come in after the law come out . . .

LEFTY G.: Sons of bitches.

JUSTICE: . . . made things worse for all. See the sign? Don't think I put that up. All those that signed it did . . . and let me tell you, it's been enforced more than once. Believe me.

VIEJO: I see no reason not to.

JUSTICE: I don't mean it that way. Everybody knows that when you fell into dealing drugs, it was because of . . .

VIEJO: Everybody knows?

JUSTICE: Well, everybody that counts.

VIEJO: Chile?

JUSTICE: Yeah . . . I guess she got ears.

VIEJO: She not?

JUSTICE: No, she's cool. Goes to college in the day, works here at night . . . she been like a daughter to me.

VIEJO: And you've been like a father.

JUSTICE: As much as a father as you would've been.

VIEJO: Vaya, that's cool.

JUSTICE: You're off for good? No extra change hanging around somewhere . . . is there?

VIEJO: Nothing hanging loose. Everything is tightened up.

JUSTICE: Max-out? All of it?

VIEJO: Every dime of it, that includes delinquent too.

JUSTICE: Well, that's really good to hear . . . Lefty G. . . .

LEFTY G.: God listens to those who speak.

VIEJO: And the devil listens to those who whisper.

JUSTICE: You remember, huh?

LEFTY G.: Two points for El Viejo.

JUSTICE: Lefty G., put a tab up for Viejo.

LEFTY G.: You got it.

JUSTICE: Had a chance to cop some combo with Chile?

VIEJO: Negative, that thing about the cracked skull was cute, but I get the feeling it would have been my head and not Lefty G's.

JUSTICE: You sell yourself too short.

VIEJO: Perhaps, quizás, pero I still feel it.

JUSTICE: It's all in your mind. You know every time someone comes out of the joint it's paranoid time.

VIEJO: Run that shit under somebody else's belt, not mine.

JUSTICE: I'll prove it to you.

VIEJO: Later . . . right now tell me why the streets are so empty of players.

JUSTICE: There are players in the streets, just that things change. Some players are not into the same kinda things we were into. You looking for a game? Or are you gonna shoot your regular.

VIEJO: I'll do some scouting first . . . before I go into the field.

JUSTICE: Hey, Chile, come here.

VIEJO: I told you later.

JUSTICE: But I thought . . .

VIEJO: You shouldn't think for me . . . I'm capable of doing my own.

JUSTICE: Okay, what is the matter? Why the rocks?

VIEJO: I haven't any rocks. Look, all I wanna find out is how is everything and everybody doing . . .

JUSTICE: Well, let me put it to you this way, Viejo. Everything is everything . . . and everybody is either breathing or not. You're scared?

VIEJO: Me? No . . . well, okay, damn it, I am.

JUSTICE: Why?

VIEJO: Look. What am I supposed to say to her? "Hi, I'm Luis Rivera. I'm the spick who turned your mother into a whore and dragged her down into drug addiction with me, into prisons and hospitals, and abandoned you to a players' bar?" I never gave her anything worth having . . .

JUSTICE: Wait a minute. If I remember correctly . . . there was a ten-thousand-dollar bank account in her name when you left her

10

in my house.

VIEJO: Your memory is beautiful, but that was only material things.

JUSTICE: What are you talking about "material things?" What else is there?

VIEJO: There's things that money can't buy, something of value . . . from the soul of love . . . something spiritual . . .

JUSTICE: From the soul of love . . . are you for real? Where the hell were you? In some prison, or a Majariji Guru retreat? What's gotten into you? This isn't the Viejo I know or knew.

VIEJO: Sometimes I wonder myself . . . I guess it's age and time. You know something? The first time we went to the joint . . . nothing . . . time slipped by so fast that I was swift and clean with my mitts . . . copped what I needed, and kept something extra just in case I ran out. This time the bit put a hurting on my ass. This time I woke up to find a very rude awakening waiting for me in the mirror.

JUSTICE: Okay. You woke up to a certain fact of life, that once meant shit to you, and means the same to millions of others . . . but she is your flesh and blood . . .

VIEJO: Jake, I don't know if I can handle it.

JUSTICE: There's only one way to find out. Right? Well?

VIEJO: Don't go too far.

JUSTICE: Fuck you . . . now straighten yourself up. . . . Chile, you got some time for yourself.

CHILE: Good, I'll go get something to eat . . . I hate the food here. (Begins to leave.)

JUSTICE: That's not what I mean . . . (She returns.) . . . Viejo would like to talk to you.

CHILE: He has nothing to say . . . anyway, not to me, Justice.

JUSTICE: He's your father.

CHILE: In name only.

JUSTICE: He needs you, Chile.

CHILE: I needed him when I was young.

JUSTICE: Chile . . . don't do that to him.

CHILE: He did it to himself. And if that's why you gave me some time off for myself . . . I'll go back to work.

JUSTICE: Go back to work . . . he's a customer. Treat him like one . . . his table is lonely . . .his glass is empty.

CHILE: Yessum bossem . . . (Cross to Viejo.)

VIEJO: Hi.

CHILE: Your glass is empty.

11

VIEJO: Sí, yo sé. ¿Cómo está mi hija?

CHILE: Sorry I don't speak Spanish.

VIEJO: Chile . . . *(Enter Jr. Balloon with Rosa.)*

JR. BALLOON: Why is there no music in this place?

JUSTICE: 'Cause we was all waiting for the rhythm to arrive.

JR. BALLOON: I am here.

JUSTICE: And there's the box. *(Motions Rosa to juke box.)*

CHILE: Customers . . .

VIEJO: Chile.

CHILE: Customers . . . see you around some time. *(Music beings. Jr. Balloon dances with Chile and Rosa.)*

JR. BALLOON: Hey, Justice . . . what do you think about this girl putting a make-believe beauty mark on her face without my permission.?

ROSA: But baby, I did it for you.

JR. BALLOON: I was talking to Justice. Girl, you been beginning to take too many liberties. . . . Girl, you keep that mouth of yours running when it should be closed, I'm gonna have to run you down to the East Side with those transvestites.

JUSTICE: The beauty mark adds essence to her beauty, Jr. Balloon.

CHILE: She should have something black about her. *(Serves drinks to everybody.)*

JR. BALLOON: Good . . . good, give the young lady two points. She's learning too much from you, Justice.

JUSTICE: Like father, like daughter. That's what some fool said.

JR. BALLOON: Go find us a nice table, Rosa.

JUSTICE: All the tables are nice, Jr. Balloon.

JR. BALLOON: What would you do without my business? *(Enter Willie Bodega with Kahlu.)*

JUSTICE: Celebrate!

WILLIE BODEGA: Lefty . . . hey, what's going on? Junior Balloon . . . Justice . . .

JR. BALLOON: Well, if it ain't the talking gringo. . . . Hit any grocery stores lately?

WILLIE BODEGA: Funny . . . funny . . . you got a nerve talking. You look more like an advertising for a macaroni clothing store.

JR. BALLOON: Poorly. Who writes your material?

WILLIE BODEGA: The same joker that made your suit. Your money's calling you.

JR. BALLOON: Yeah, but there's no police thirty-eights coming from that moneymaker.

12

WILLIE BODEGA: Lefty, let me have . . .

LEFTY G.: You can have anything and as many as you want . . .the tab is on Cat Eyes.

WILLIE BODEGA: Well, in that case, let me have a bottle of your best champagne.

JR. BALLOON: You mean to tell me you let me put money on the counter?

LEFTY G.: You always said you got it like the feds . . .

JR. BALLOON: Yeah, but when it's free? And the competition is paying? Well, that's another story all together.

JUSTICE: You should never acknowledge competition, Jr. Balloon; can slow you down worrying about it.

JR. BALLOON: Who worries? The way I see it, there's enough for everyone that can handle it.

WILLIE BODEGA: No one gives Jr. Balloon any compo.

JR. BALLOON: You tell 'em, whitey. June, the month of love. Love, the bug you just can't slap away.

WILLIE BODEGA: California? This is the best? How we gonna toast with grape juice? (Pop! Piano fanfare.) Here's to the hustle. (Fanfare.)

JR. BALLOON: And the hustlers. (Fanfare.)

VIEJO: And to the suckers.

WILLIE BODEGA: The suckers.

VIEJO: Who without there would be no hustle . . . or hustlers.

JR. BALLOON: Suck my left nut. Am I seeing who I'm seeing? Viejo.

VIEJO: Jr. . . . Willie . . . long time. I see you two are still on each other's cases.

WILLIE BODEGA: Can't shake the snake charmer loose.

WILLIE BODEGA: We didn't steal it. We took it.

JR. BALLOON: You and your brother should have never stolen my lunch money. Justice, you ain't shit. You stand there, knowing the old man is in town, and don't let up on it. . . . Shit . . .

JUSTICE: The toilet is that way.

JR. BALLOON: What are you doing, old man?

VIEJO: Well, nothing as of yet, just looking over the store.

WILLIE BODEGA: You got ends?

VIEJO: Got enough to see me over any humps . . .

JR. BALLOON: How's your collar?

VIEJO: My collar is tighter than a pimp's hatband.

JR. BALLOON: I'll have it loosen for you tonight . . . Rosa, come here, mama. *(Cross Rosa to Jr. who motions, turns her towards Viejo. Rosa crosses to Viejo.)*

ROSA: Hi.

JR. BALLOON: This here is one fine, moneymaking 'ho'e . . . most of the bread I made with her head. Just give her your address and she is yours for as long as it takes . . . but remember, just for that long, not longer than that.

VIEJO: She young.

JR. BALLOON: She old enough. Can you handle it, mama?

ROSA: Anything you say . . . but he old.

JR. BALLOON: Don't let snow fool you, there plenty of oil in the basement. *(Laughs.)*

WILLIE BODEGA: Jesus H. Christ! Jr. Balloon, you tell the corniest jokes . . . and then he laughs at them too. I don't see what they see . . .

JR. BALLOON: Mama, tell this near-sighted fool what you see in Jr.

ROSA: June.

JR. BALLOON: And that's all they wanna see, 'cause they don't wanna see the winter in me. . . . Okay, mama, go back there and look pretty.

ROSA: Old man, when I get through with you, you'll be in your second childhod.

JR. BALLOON: That's why you could never make it as a Mack . . . you never let a woman see what she wants to see, but what you want her to see. This way, she is always looking for something to see.

VIEJO: "I see," said the blind man . . . to his deaf daughter.

WILLIE BODEGA: I know this payroll clerk who's given me all the details of his route. He has pocket money for both of us . . . ten G's apiece.

VIEJO: Is it a two-man job?

WILLIE BODEGA: Sure.

VIEJO: Your word?

WILLIE BODEGA: No, not really, but you know things sometimes happen, and . . .

VIEJO: No thanks . . . I don't play alarm clock.

WILLIE BODEGA: Just trying to be helpful.

VIEJO: I know, thank you, but I am not looking for welfare.

WILLIE BODEGA: Excuse me for living . . . shit!

JR. BALLOON: Why be like that, old man? He only trying to be helpful . . . he's a heist kid, that's all he knows.

VIEJO: You're right, I don't know where my head was there. . . . Excuse me, I'll go apologize . . . Willie, look, I didn't mean to sound like that.

WILLIE BODEGA: That's okay . . . I was out of line, but you did teach me everything I know about the business.

VIEJO: Let me buy you a drink.

WILLIE BODEGA: Haven't you heard? The drinks are on Cat Eyes.

CAT EYES: Hold it! Hold it! Wait a minute. Now . . . what's this about the drinks on me? I don't remember ever inviting you to drink with me.

JUSTICE: Well, you invited everybody for an hour of free drinks tonight.

PHEBE: They are running the bar on you, Papi.

CAT EYES: Running the bar on me? Justice, you must be clear out of your mind . . . I ain't paying for nobody's drinks . . .

JUSTICE: Cat Eyes, there are many unwritten rules in the game that you play . . . this is a hustler's place . . . all my customers are players, and they go with the rules . . . the same ones that are out in the street apply here. One . . . the major, is respect . . . you don't disrespect the place . . . if you turn your back on the bar you disrespect me . . . and if you disrespect . . . you pay.

CAT EYES: I have never placed my back on the bar.

JUSTICE: She did . . . she's yours . . . you're responsible.

CAT EYES: You didn't tell me this. You embarrassed me in front of all these people. Get out . . . and I don't want to see you at home. I want you in them streets until yours soles waste. Get out. Beat it. (*Turns to Justice.*) Here's a couple of hundred, Justice, this should cover it.

JUSTICE: Man, goddam you young. Look here, brotherman, it has nothing to do with the bread, can't you get that through your head? You ain't cool at all, are you? I mean, you need some type of schooling, man. If you don't get your head together, you gonna end up with a teacher.

CAT EYES: Yeah, who?

JUSTICE: Me . . . I make a good principal, brotherman.

CAT EYES: And I never made a good student.

WILLIE BODEGA: That's why you a dropout in the players' game.

JR. BALLOON: Pendejito . . . asshole.

CAT EYES: Oye, tú no me conoce' a mí. You don't know me.

JR. BALLOON: And I don't really want to either, bro.

WILLIE BODEGA: Man, you ain't got no kind of class, do you?

CAT EYES: Who the fuck is this fucking gringo talking to?

WILLIE BODEGA: Unless you a wall, motherfucker, I'm talking to you.

CAT EYES: Better dig yourself, mister. (*Cat Eyes reaches inside jacket.*)

WILLIE BODEGA: You do right calling me mister.

JR. BALLOON: Better not go for it, kid.

WILLIE BODEGA: Guess at your age you wanna call it a game of cards.

JUSTICE: Willie Bodega . . .

WILLIE BODEGA: Yeah, Justice, I'm cool, man, I'm cool.

CAT EYES: He better be or he be dead soon. You dig?

WILLIE BODEGA: (*Going for gun. Everyone clears.*) Now, where have I heard that rap before?

JUSTICE: Junior . . . Willie . . . I mean it.

WILLIE BODEGA: Okay, Willie B. ain't gonna cause you no damages.

CHILE: Look, if you ain't gonna put no money on the tab, then book out of here.

CAT EYES: Okay, I take the tab . . . I can afford it. (*Staring at Willie.*)

JUSTICE: You can't afford it.

LEFTY G.: Well, what you gonna do, young blood? You stare real hard.

WILLIE BODEGA: He must practice . . . in front of the mirror.

JR. BALLOON: Come on . . . sit down already, Willie . . . leave the dude now.

WILLIE BODEGA: I ain't bothering him.

CAT EYES: Your breath is.

WILLIE BODEGA: Oh my, oh my . . . next thing he gonna do is talk about my mother. Oh my, oh my . . . I feel so rotten, boo hoo . . . I'll weep for days behind that statement.

JR. BALLOON: Willie . . .

WILLIE BODEGA: Yeah, okay, Junior.

JR. BALLOON: Man, it ain't you I'm worrying about, man, it's Justice's place, man . . . you know the place is hot.

WILLIE BODEGA: Look, man, I'm gonna squash this here bullshit between me and you, kid . . . but I just wonna drop something on you before I do squash it.

CAT EYES: Make it short.

WILLIE BODEGA: As short as it takes, man. Man, if you wanna be a player, you got to realize that everything that jumps your way ain't threatening your manhood, brotherman.

CAT EYES: A whitey that raps like a nigger. Ain't that something?

WILLIE BODEGA: No, that ain't nothing, man. I just rap this way cuz that the way I raps . . .but what I wanna tell you is this, young blood . . . the man been in the game before you crawls out of your mama's cunt, and this man told you, rightly so too, that your lady disrespected the place, and there was no kind of shit jumping your way, man. All you had to do, if you really think yourself as being what you are, a man, is, man, that you apologize to the place and accept the play, man, to you . . . that's all. No big thing . . . no big money coming out of your pocket . . . no big thing being taken out of your hustle, man. Nothing, man, nothing at all . . . but you gotta jump stink right quick on the place, because you think everybody is out to make you or take something away from you. That's too bad, man . . .cuz you ain't never gonna learn to trust, man, and that's real bad . . .cuz if you can't trust, then you can't ever relax and enjoy the stings you make. Can you dig it, man? And you wanna know something? The run of the tab on you was just a way of Justice letting you know that you blew it in here with him and that you should be aware of it. Like on the streets a knife in your gut or a bullet in your head would have been the respond and I guess that's what you think that you are supposed to respect, the force, and fuck the rest of the real attitude.

CAT EYES: Man, you talk too much.

WILLIE BODEGA: I guess that I do, 'cause I like you and your motherfucking arrogance.

JUSTICE: Man, brotherman, you better believe that he likes you for reasons known only to him.

CAT EYES: Maybe he's a faggot.

JUSTICE: You want your table?

CAT EYES: Yeah.

CHILE: It's ready. (Cross Lefty with drinks on tray.)

JR. BALLOON: Hey, Lefty . . . can you dance, man?

LEFTY G.: Sure.

VIEJO: So that's what out here on the streets making the money, huh?

JUSTICE: Yeah, that's what out here, man. That ain't nothing. Wait till you see the rest parading around, man.

DIAMOND: Man, Justice, I . . . I . . . man, tell me something quick, man, like . . . like this dude, man . . . I'm gonna waste the motherfucker, I'm gonna waste the motherfucker.

MAN: That'll be the last motherfucker you'll ever try to waste too. (*Diamond angrily heads toward Man, but Justice restrains him.*)

JUSTICE: Man, calm down, man, calm down . . . like, what the hell, man. (*Diamond calms down a bit and walks around acknowledging everyone.*)

DIAMOND: Who that?

JUSTICE: This here is Viejo, man, a really down to the . . .

DIAMOND: That's the dude you be rappin' about, man? Hey, what's happening?

VIEJO: Right now you're what's happening, brotherman.

DIAMOND: Thank you.

JUSTICE: Now, who is this that you gonna kill this time, man?

WILLIE BODEGA: He's always killing somebody.

DIAMOND: No, this time I'm for real, Willie, really for real, man. You know what this dude did outside to me . . . to me, Diamond Ring, the baddest Mack-O-Roni that ever jumped out of the cooker. This dude out there sold me a motherfucking . . . a motherfucking wolf ticket in front to my woman, man, in front of my ladies. See, Willie? This time is serious business . . .

WILLIE BODEGA: Yeah, man, real serious.

DIAMOND: Him and his boys.

WILLIE BODEGA: You ain't got no piece, man?

DIAMOND: Have you ever known me to wake up without brushing my teeth with my three roscoes?

WILLIE BODEGA: Then why are you in here rappin' about it?

DIAMOND: Man, this dude, this punk, called me out in front of the motherfucking cops . . . in front of the cops, man. That's why I'm here, man, cuz or else . . . you know what it all about, man. Man, I got to get my feelings out or else I be out there with these two dudes dead at my feet, facing the motherfucking police, man, and you know about me, man, I hold court in the streets, man, I can't do no time.

CAT EYES: That's why people worry about him knowing too much.

DIAMOND: You talking 'bout me?

JUSTICE: That kind of talk is not allowed here, mister.

CAT EYES: It's a free country.

JUSTICE: Since when?

WILLIE BODEGA: Be cool, Diamond. He's a little hot cuz Justice is running the bar on him.

DIAMOND: Give me four bottles of the best champagne that you got, Just.

CAT EYES: That's the only way you can get it . . .when it's free.

DIAMOND: Make it eight.

JUSTICE: No, man, you can't do that.

DIAMOND: Why not?.

JUSTICE: You ain't gonna drink them, man, that's why . . . and I hate seeing good champagne going to waste.

DIAMOND: I'll drink them, besides, I got friends that will help me. *(Everyone tinkles their glasses.)*

JUSTICE: Oh, shit, here we go with another drunk. . . . Lefty, give Diamond a bottle of champagne.

LEFTY G.: Right.

DIAMOND: Oooh, come on, Justice, my pockets grow hungry out there. I mean, if you gonna give away welfare . . . give me some.

LEFTY G.: Hey, Diamond . . . you did right, man, walking away. There will be another time.

JUSTICE: There always is, remember that, there always is, another time.

DIAMOND: I will, cuz I believe it, man.

CHILE: Your table is ready, Diamond.

DIAMOND: Thank you. *(Looks at Cat Eyes and kisses Chile.)* Show me the way. Hey, Old man, care to drink with me? *(Enter Kahlu from ladies room.)*

VIEJO: No thank you, young blood.

DIAMOND: Suit yourself.

CAT EYES: Hey, baby.

CHILE: My name is Chile.

CAT EYES: Come here, girl.

CHILE: What do you want, sir?

CAT EYES: Hey, man, come on . . . don't do that to me.

CHILE: The way I see it you are doing it to yourself.

CAT EYES: Come on, baby, be nice.

CHILE: Have you ever seen me be mean?

CAT EYES: What do you call what you are doing to me being?

CHILE: Natural.

CAT EYES: Hate to see you in the mornings.

CHILE: Really?

CAT EYES: Now, what the hell did I do to receive this treatment?

CHILE: You don't know?

CAT EYES: Girl, if I did I wouldn't be asking, now would I?

19

CHILE: Can never tell about you.

CAT EYES: Now, what is that suppose to mean?

CHILE: Just what I said, that's all.

CAT EYES: Come, baby, sit down for a second with me, let's rap this here thing out between you and me real nice and quiet-like.

CHILE: I'm working.

CAT EYES: Take some time off . . .

JUSTICE: Chile, you gonna host or you gonna play the host?

CHILE: I have some time for myself, remember you said so.

JUSTICE: Yeah . . .

CHILE: What you got to say to me? It better be good.

CAT EYES: Now why does it have to be good? You act like I'm suppose to always drop a line on you if I want your attention.

CHILE: Your behavior tonight was enough to grab anyone's attention.

CAT EYES: Oh, is that it?

CHILE: Yes, that's it.

CAT EYES: Listen, I can't let these older dudes try to run over me. Most of them think that 'cause they been out on this thing longer than god, man, they think they are self-appointed teachers of the play. Everyone and their mother wants to run a school for P.I.'s. Ain't that a kick in the ass?

CHILE: Carlos . . .

CAT EYES: Don't call me Carlos here . . . I'm sorry baby.

CHILE: That's okay, Cat Eyes.

CAT EYES: Come baby. Why the ice? . . . melt, baby, melt on me . . . I get enough cold weather in them streets, baby, don't you start snowing on me too.

CHILE: I'm sorry, baby.

CAT EYES: How about a kiss?

CHILE: Not in here . . . Justice will blow a fuse.

CAT EYES: You said he ain't your father . . . not your real father.

CHILE: Oh, but he is . . . as real as any other girl's father is to them.

CAT EYES: Okay, baby, but I don't like playing high school boyfriend.

CHILE: I ain't asking you to play anything at all.

CAT EYES: Let's squash the whole thing and let me rap to you seriously, baby.

CHILE: I'm always listening to you.

CAT EYES: Like I told you last time, baby, I want out but I need me to make some money. I don't wanna work in no place for some lousey weekly salary that costs you your fucking life, baby, that's not for me. No, I needs something more of value than that, baby

. . . I need to go on for about a year. And then you know what I wanna do, baby? I wanna open up something like this, to be cool just like Justice is. I mean something that brings you respect as well as a decent living, as I know living to be. Like you know what I mean, baby? Do I make any kind of sense to you, baby?

CHILE: You sound like Viejo.

CAT EYES: The Viejo?

CHILE: That's him over there.

CAT EYES: Shit, a legend in person. You know him?

CHILE: Yeah, I do.

CAT EYES: Shit, now from him I wouldn't mind being schooled . . . though he don't look like much to me.

CHILE: People change their ways over the years, Papi.

CAT EYES: So I've been told.

CHILE: Baby . . .

CAT EYES: Yeah, you know him, huh? Maybe you could introduce me to him, real cool like. You know what I mean?

CHILE: Baby, I don't want to introduce you to somebody like that.

CAT EYES: A minute ago you sounded like you admired him.

CHILE: Maybe I do, but I also hate him with a passion . . . I wish he were dead . . .

CAT EYES: That's kind of a strong wish for a beautiful girl like you.

CHILE: Well, maybe not dead, but in the joint doing life where he belongs.

CAT EYES: You only wish for the best.

CHILE: Baby, let's drop him. Let's talk about us. (*Kisses Cat Eyes.*)

CAT EYES: Yeah, we never get enough time. Baby, I . . . I wanna open up a classy stable of girls that'll make these guys eyes pop out of their motherfucking . . . skulls. (*Cross Junior and Rosa to their table.*) You know, girls with style . . . a private business . . . and I can do it, but I need your help, baby, I really need your help, baby. Please don't do that, baby, listen to me. Don't turn off on me . . . please, baby, listen to what I got to say first.

CHILE: I'm listening.

CAT EYES: No, you're not.

CHILE: Make it quick.

CAT EYES: I'll make it short . . . good-bye.

CHILE: What?

CAT EYES: I said, "I'll see you around sometime, baby."

CHILE: Carlos.

CAT EYES: Later, baby later. (*Crosses to Viejo.*) Hi . . . Cat Eyes is my name.

VIEJO: Hi.

CAT EYES: Can I buy you a drink?

VIEJO: You already have.

CAT EYES: Yeah, that's right . . . you're welcome.

VIEJO: I didn't thank you.

CAT EYES: No, you didn't.

VIEJO: And I wasn't planning to either.

CAT EYES: What's the matter . . . you don't like me or something.

VIEJO: It's not a matter of whether I like you or not. Even if I didn't, would that make a big difference in your life?

CAT EYES: Not one bit of a difference, I was around before I met you and I'll be around after you hit that grass in the cemetery. You wanna blow?

VIEJO: No thanks, man, really. I just got out and I'm trying to figure something out in my head for myself, first, before I make any kind of moves in any direction that ain't considered legal by the state. Dig what I mean?

CAT EYES: Yeah, that you is leary like a motherfucker.

VIEJO: That's a good lesson for a young blood like you to learn. When you are leary, you are careful . . . if you're careful, you survive in this here planet. If you take that into your brain for a moment each day, young blood, and with a little bit of luck, you might live to be my age.

CAT EYES: I hope I never get that old. (Crosses to his table.)

VIEJO: That's just the same thing I said a long time ago. (Cross Justice to Veijo's table. Sits down.)

JUSTICE: So you met Cat Eyes.

VIEJO: No, he met me.

CAT EYES: That's what they all say.

DIAMOND: You know something, Junior? Like, some people think they are players, you know what I mean? They really think they can do this here thing that we call the game . . . like they get themselves a couple of junkie broads, put them on the corner with a million kinds of disease dropping out of their eyes, as well as their cunts, like gonorrhea, syphillis . . . they buy themselves a flashy suit, from some wholesale store on Broadway, and jump into the scene calling themselves P.I.'s. Man, they ain't never seen a pimp unless they were shining his motherfucking shoes.

CAT EYES: Fuck you, punk motherfucker.

DIAMOND: What's with the kid? Oh, you want to fuck me, kid?

22

Maybe I should be out on the corner. (*Various other ab-libs.*)

JR. BALLOON: How should I now, man? Maybe he's crazy or something.

DIAMOND: Must be.

LEFTY G.: You okay, Cat Eyes? (*Crosses to men's room.*)

DIAMOND: He probably had too much to drink . . . you know these young dudes, can't handle the firewater.

JUSTICE: Chile, get me a clean glass, will you?

CHILE: Can't you get it yourself?

JUSTICE: Yes, I could, but I asked you. Didn't I.

CHILE: You lazy motherfucker, you fat lazy . . . (*Various other ab-libs. Crosses to table.*)

JUSTICE: Shut up already, will you? Man, all day you been quibbering with the jibbering. Girl, I mean like, I don't know where you get all that from 'cause it don't come from your papa, that's for sure, and it don't come from you mama and you can ask your papa about that.

CHILE: How would he know?

VIEJO: I did love her, Chile. In my own way, I loved your mother.

CHILE: Sure, I bet.

JUSTICE: How much?

CHILE: His life . . . here . . . (*Slams drink on table.*)

JUSTICE: Thank you . . . maybe if you banged it a little harder it could've broken and then you could start . . .

CHILE: Up yours.

JUSTICE: Is that for my health or my death?

CHILE: Either way you want it.

JUSTICE: Strong girl, ain't she?

VIEJO: Yeah, she is a strong woman.

JUSTICE: See you in a little while. I'm gonna talk with her.

VIEJO: Okay, later. (*Enter Bam-Bam, followed by Satisfaction. Bam-Bam gives wallet to Satisfaction and hides. Satisfaction takes money out of wallet and gives it to Diamond Ring and goes to lounge. Enter a Salesman, looks around and heads for lounge. Diamond Ring follows. Bam-Bam leaves.*)

ROSA: Are you ready to go, old man?

VIEJO: In a little while, girl, in a little while. Let me finish my drink first. O.K.?

ROSA: Take your time . . . Junior said my only work today is you.

VIEJO: Tell Junior I really appreciate it.

ROSA: I will, old man.

VIEJO: Hey, Rosa.

ROSA: Yeah?

VIEJO: Stop calling me old man . . . the name is Viejo.

ROSA: Viejo.

VIEJO: Right . . . (*Salesman comes from lounge. Picks up wallet. Cashes check and leaves.*)

JR. BALLOON: Rosa, come here girl, dance with me.

WILLIE BODEGA: What make you think you can dance?

JR. BALLOON: If you believed it hard enough, you might be able to get up on the floor too with a young lady wrapped in your arms. Right, Rosa?

ROSA: Anything you say, daddy.

WILLIE BODEGA: Man, I'm gonna have to shut this man's mouth all up. Now you gonna look mighty silly, man. Come here girl . . .

DIAMOND: We got something going here.

WILLIE BODEGA: (*Handing his guns to Lefty.*) If I lose, shoot him. (*Kahlu dances to Willie.*) . . . Diamond, put on a record with a hustle to it.

JR. BALLOON: Man, put on some hot Latin.

WILLIE BODEGA: Shit, man, that don't scare me none at all.

JR. BALLOON: Okay, loosen up. (*He turns music off.*)

LEFTY G.: You know how this whitey got the name Willie Bodega?

DIAMOND: Yeah, Lefty, we know.

ROSA: I don't.

LEFTY G.: Could I tell you then? Junior, can I tell her?

JR. BALLOON: Man, we are about to have the dance contest of the century and you wanna tell her a dumb thing like that . . .

LEFTY G.: It ain't dumb . . .

JR. BALLOON: It's about as dumb and dull a story as you are, Lefty.

LEFTY G.: I'm sorry, I won't say anything.

DIAMOND: Hey Lefty . . . Lefty Gorilla . . .

JR. BALLOON: Go tell Rosa how he got his name.

LEFTY G.: You mean it?

JR. BALLOON: Of course, man, of course, man, I was just fucking with your head before . . . after you tell it, we'll have the dance contest. Is that cool with you, Willie B?

WILLIE BODEGA: That's cool with me . . . I always like listening as to how I became a spick.

LEFTY G.: You know, Rosa, before you was born we all use to hang out together as kids. Right, fellas? . . . me and Justice are like that. Right, Justice?

JUSTICE: Right.

LEFTY G.: Yeah, man, it was the good old days. We started together
doing everything, man, it was real cool. Like Justice and me, we
would go to these places. Right? In uniforms of cleaning people
. . . and nobody would say anything to us and after the place was
empty we would go into the offices and Justice would yell out.
"All those that wanna live, hit the floor. All those what wanna
go to meet their maker remain on your feet." And the whole
place be on the floor before you could blink your eyes . . . man, it
was real cool. After we got some money we started doing other
things. Like Justice became a big numbers man. Man, it was real
cool.

JR. BALLOON: Man, I don't think Justice would like you talking
like that out here in the open, man, tú sabe'?

LEFTY G.: We are among friends. Ain't we?

DIAMOND: Yeah, Lefty, that's true . . . but you know walls have
ears and you guys did a lot of shit that ain't accounted for yet.

LEFTY G.: Yeah, that makes sense. Yeah. Well, you Rosa . . .
sometimes you are traveling so high on the hog that you forget
where you are or who you are and how you got to where you are.
That's what happened to all of us within a couple of years; we
were doing it so hard in those days that we forgot to be cool about
ourselves, man, like we just didn't think and the next thing you
know, we were all in Attica on 36 gallery. The fuck ups . . . that's
what they say, man, we were getting over, wasn't we? . . . we sure
was, man, we sure was. I use to cook and play bodyguard to the
fellas and their young chickens, you know. These dudes were
doing it up. Anyway, hard times always fall on all of us, sooner or
later hard times are gonna fall and at that time we all looked out
for one another. Right, fellas? We sure did, all that time. I
remember the time we had to throw this guy off the tier becuz he
thought we were fooling with him. Man, he swam in the air just
like people swim in the water. It was really funny. Man I had
some real nice times in the joint in them days . . . I sure did. I had
better times and friends in the joint than I ever did in the streets
. . . in my life . . . in any place I ever went. When hard times fell
on us we would look out for one another and all you had to do was
say, "Hey, hard times are here for the brother," and we all knew
better days would come . . . we all knew better days would come
. . . and better days would come . . . right around the corner.

. . . And you know . . . I was never . . . no, that's not what I want to say. *(Begins to leave.)*

ROSA: Lefty, Willie . . . Willie. *(Everyone coaxes him on.)*

LEFTY G.: Willie . . . Willie . . . oye, Willie, mira, Willie . . . let me cop some sugar . . . Willie me and you on the sandwich, man . . . Willie you got some matches? And Willie, would say, man, you think this is welfare . . . Willie, you making some cool aid tonight? Me and you bro, just like it always been, me and you brother, me and you. And Willie say, "You motherfucker must think I'm a fucking Bodega."

WILLIE BODEGA: Goddam corner store.

LEFTY G.: Willie "Z GALLERY" Bodega. Willie Bodega that's how he got his name. Me and Willie, we used to play handball for money. Money is cigarettes, you know, or he would have me fight some dude in the yard for money. You know? I use to fight real good, I could have been pro . . . you know I could have been pro, Right, Willie? . . . that's what they all said, I could have been pro. *(Fights with Diamond Ring. Gets out of hand. Justice stops him.)* Yeah, those were the good old days. Justice says we now are into the good new days. That's funny, ain't it? I mean the way Willie Bodega got his name.

DIAMOND: That's funny, Lefty . . . real funny.

LEFTY G.: You know something, I wasn't going to say this before, but I will now. When I was in the joint with them . . . I was never lonely . . . *(Crosses to bar.)*

DIAMOND: Let's have the dance. *(Jr. Balloon turns music back on.)*

CAT EYES: Man, that dude is a head blower.

VIEJO: You know something, Cat Eyes? Your experience is very limited.

CAT EYES: You got the same type of attitude the rest of these niggers have. You think you know it all.

VIEJO: I know that there's a lot I don't know . . . and I also know that the only way I am going to learn the things I need to know is if I admit that I need to know these things.

CAT EYES: You sure must have done a lot of time in the joint. When I was in the joint, all the long-time-doing motherfuckers talk like you talk, man.

VIEJO: And how is that?

CAT EYES: Like they see things.

VIEJO: That's because they did. And I bet you saw nothing in what they saw. Right?

26

CAT EYES: Right. They all talk nonsense.

VIEJO: That's too bad. That is why you think the way you do now.

CAT EYES: I think all right and I do all right too.

VIEJO: Not in the circle you don't, I can feel it and I am here fresh off the banana boat.

CAT EYES: Look, man, I don't care what them motherfuckers think about me and my game, I'm getting over. That's what counts. I pay my bills and eat good food . . . and I fuck everynight.

VIEJO: So does the warden.

CAT EYES: Man, let me tell you something.

VIEJO: Something I don't know? . . . something that has meaning? Or the "I told the 'ho'e to sell the kid but keep the Cadillac cuz I need the wheels to move," kinda shit?

CAT EYES: You see them dudes? They think they got it made.

VIEJO: Don't you?

CAT EYES: They got some of it made, but not all of it. They got themselves years ahead of me in the game . . . plenty of time in the life to learn much experience. But me, I came fast, Viejo, faster than any of them. That's why they don't like me, cuz they all know that I'm swifter than any of them were at my age, man. I am a young blood fresh off the doctor's mitts. You know I still have the smell of the afterbirth hanging about me . . . but I'm swifter than those people who call themselves "folks," and have the smell of death in the breath. Me? I am new life, Viejo, I am new life. You think I don't know they are jealous of me and my fast talking self. Man. I know that. Shit, that is why I talk to them the way I do cuz I know that. You think I may be wrong, but I'm not . . . I'm not . . . Viejo, my rap is strong and my words are never wrong. I'm young and faster than a streak of lightning and a ball of heat . . . and I always land on my feet . . . ever since I could remember I never touched the floor with my knees. You see that girl, Chile, they all wanted her but they all fear Justice and Lefty Gorilla, but not me cuz their time is up on the earth. I know that his is a jungle law . . . (Enter Bam-Bam and Satisfaction.) and I'm steaking my name to that game. She is gonna make me a very wealthy man, my man. She is gonna put me on the mack map of the year . . . every year until dooms day.

VIEJO: Are you saying what I think you are saying?

CAT EYES: That's right, mister. I'm gonna turn her sweet ass out.

VIEJO: I can't let you do that.

CAT EYES: What you mean you can't let me do that? Who the fuck are you? Oh, you wanna turn her out there for yourself. Is that it?

VIEJO: You don't seem to understand. She isn't going out to the way of all flesh.

CAT EYES: You don't seem to understand you can't stop me cuz she loves me . . . and besides . . . why the fuck are you telling me some shit like that if you don't want her as a pimp? Why the fuck are you playing boy scout?

VIEJO: I'm her father. (*Montage. Activity of bar takes over, dancing, ad-libs, music building to end of Act One. Freeze.*)

ACT II

SCENE 1. A small hotel room.

ROSA: Come, Papi . . . get it on. Oh, Papi, get it on . . . come on, baby. Shit, wait a fucking minute, man . . . what's happening, old man? We been in this damn bed for a half an hour and all you be doing is slobbering all over me . . . and your johnson ain't even hard. What's the matter, man? Are you too old to get it up any more?

VIEJO: Shut up, bitch.

ROSA: Oh, now it's the shut up bitch routine. Huh? What you gonna do, old man? Ha . . . look at this . . . it's as dead as a corpse in the city morgue. So what you gonna do, Mister Viejo? . . . the master of the hustle . . . what you gonna do? Hey, what's the matter? The cat got your tongue? You lost your voice as well as your strength to do it? Shit, I lay in the bed and I get a tongue bath . . . man I can dig a little tongue, but too much of it makes me horny, honey, and you shouldn't be out here giving up all this tongue if you can't give up anything else . . . I don't wanna be sucked off like a lesbian, I wanna be fucked like a woman.

VIEJO: You going too far with your mouth, who'e.

ROSA: Not as far as you went with yours, old man.

VIEJO: Stop calling me old man. You know my name.

ROSA: Yes, Viejo, which means old man in Spanish.

VIEJO: . . . In Spanish not in English.

ROSA: Does that rule also go for your fucking abilities?

VIEJO: What you talking about?

ROSA: That you can fuck in Spanish but not in English? (*Grabs her trying somehow by violence to retain his sexual potency. She fights then lays back and laughs.*)

VIEJO: Shit . . . god damn it . . .

ROSA: I guess that it's true what I hear the folks rappin' about men who spent most of their lives behind bars. They become nothing with their dicks, No dick Ricks . . . can't get it uppers . . . unless the other person is a young boy like Cat Eyes, huh? I saw the way you stared at him before we left the bar . . . I bet if he was in this room with you, you'd be jumping with joy . . . happier than a faggot in Boys Town. What's your score, old man . . . little boys or little girls . . . ?

VIEJO: Shut the fuck up, bitch. I said shut the fuck up. (*Grabs pillow beats her.)*

ROSA: Go on, hit me some more. . . . That's your speed, you like beating up on women. . . . Now, look, it ain't even hard . . . ah . . . aha . . . oh, that's not your speed either. Is it? Maybe you like being whipped. I've got a nice leather whip. I'll look. Here. What you want me to wear, freak? . . . black rubber suits? . . . silk stockings? . . . leather boots? . . . what ever is your pleasure I can do it . . .

VIEJO: Why the fuck are you so down on me? Don't you understand?

ROSA: Sure, I understand . . . I understand that you pretend to be what you ain't, a bad motherfucking player. . . . Maybe I should piss in a bottle or shit on your chest?

VIEJO: Bitch, I'll kill you . . . nobody speaks to me like that and lives man or woman. I'll kill you.

ROSA: Please . . . please don't kill me. I'm sorry. I'm sorry . . . please don't kill me, I wanna live. Please don't kill me.

VIEJO: Why the hell did you talk to me like that for? Who the fuck do you think I am? A motherfucking trick you picked up on the streets? I'm VIEJO . . . VIEJO. Say it, bitch, say VIEJO.

ROSA: Viejo . . . please, I didn't mean nothing . . . I only thought that you might be like Junior in bed.

VIEJO: What the hell are you talking about?

ROSA: Junior.

VIEJO: What about Junior?

ROSA: He can't do anything unless you insult him . . . unless you make him feel like he ain't shit . . .

VIEJO: That's Junior, that's not Viejo. Viejo is Viejo. Junior is Junior. If Junior is a freak for shit like that, that doesn't mean that every player in the life is the same way. Now get that through you head, cuz the next man you do that kinda shit to may not be like Viejo. I'm a nice guy, but I don't like being talked to or treated like if I was a piece of shit. Do you understand, bitch? Do you understand, bitch? Answer me.

ROSA: Yes I understand . . . I understand, Viejo.

VIEJO: Cuz it don't mean shit to me to take you off the census . . . you be one less the pussy posse will be missing on their rounds on who'e stroll. You get me?

ROSA: Yes, I do . . . please don't kill me.

VIEJO: I ain't gonna kill you . . . just lay back and shut the fuck up. I don't wanna even hear you breathe hard.

ROSA: Yes, Viejo, whatever you say.

VIEJO: Yes, Viejo, whatever you say. Now I'm the law, huh? Now I become god to you because I was willing to ice you, huh? You ain't even worth fucking if I could get it up, bitch. I ain't gonna run you that this is the first time this happened to me story, cuz it ain't. You're young and you don't understand that it's the blood that makes it hard up.

ROSA: I learned that in Sex Education.

VIEJO: Well, they should've educated you to the terrible shit you could do to a man's head by pulling that, "you can't get it up" shit on him. . . . You can ruin a man that way. Don't Junior teach you any compassion for the tricks that can't get it up?

ROSA: All Junior is interested in is how much I make.

VIEJO: That ain't the Junior I knew . . .

ROSA: He's trying to make enough money to retire like Justice did. . . . He wants out of the life and he's taking me with him. That's why I work more tricks than any of the other girls . . . that's why I know he gonna make it, cuz with me it's real feeling that pour out of him in bed. I am the one who gets it hard for him before he fucks any of the other girls, cuz I know what makes him make it move. I know him . . .

VIEJO: You wanna drink? (*Gives bottle to Rosa who drinks it straight down.*)

ROSA: Thank you . . .

VIEJO: What you know about the kid, Cat Eyes?

ROSA: Wow, for a minute there you sounded like a cop.

VIEJO: Forget about what I sound like, just talk to me.

ROSA: Okay. I'll talk to you . . . but why do you want to know about Cat Eyes? I'll tell you even if you tell me to mind my own business and answer your questions.

VIEJO: What difference would it make, then, since you just gave me the right to advise you to go fuck yourself or to give you a lie?

ROSA: The difference would be up here, in my head, in my feelings about myself. You see, Viejo, no matter what I am, how I get over . . . I like feeling good about myself . . . and if I do or say something which might make me feel bad about myself, I become very upset and I can't work. And I need to work to make that money so that Junior can retire young enough to be a part of a world that left him behind.

VIEJO: And you say that to say what? Am I expected to bring tears to my eyes and a light touch in my face?

ROSA: I don't like being a rat.

31

VIEJO: Yeah . . . right . . . okay . . . I may have to kill him.

ROSA: You may have to stand in line.

VIEJO: You can't see the truth. Can you?

ROSA: It may be the truth, but there's plenty of feelings like that around him.

VIEJO: No . . . those feelings are nothing more than just that. Feelings of hate and anger . . . but there's no feeling with me. I mean serious business when I talk of killing someone. . . . There's nothing cheap about life, Rosa . . .

ROSA: He's my brother . . .

VIEJO: Your brother?

ROSA: Yes, my brother and he was my pimp and my lover . . . until Junior came into my life.

VIEJO: I have nothing to ask you.

ROSA: He's not bad. He's not mean . . . he's trying to make a hustle. Ever since he saw Mom fucking with the welfare investigator . . . ever since then, he always jumped on what came his way and I was naturally in the world that was in his way to put to use. A very simple story of life is what Cat Eyes is about. A what can I call it? A ghetto fairy tale that came true. Are you going to kill him?

VIEJO: Yes, I am going to kill Cat Eyes . . . the pimp . . .

ROSA: You're going to waste him . . . ?

VIEJO: I'm only going to do what man has done for centuries and what others have avoided doing . . . what every player and hustler know they must do when they enter a new town or a new prison. You stop the action before it starts . . . you go for broke in any situation that threatens to take control of your game or take control of something you consider valuable enough to fight and live for. You never trade what you need to feel good in the morning about for a friendly smile from the next player because that's what keeps you going . . . what makes everything in the streets . . . the hustle, the stake . . . everything . . . worth throwing yourself under the gun everyday. Every player is a poet . . . an actor . . . a statesman . . . a priest . . . but most of all he's a player. You go out there on that street and you meet the world of suckers . . . the world of greed and whatever other names have been defined for those that seek something outside the acceptances of their society . . . and you stand with your balls exposed in this jungle of fear . . . and you battle . . . and you fight the hardest fight of your life, each day out there in them streets that demand blood to nourish its own energies . . . today and tomorrow, and all the todays and tomorrows that are left inside your soul. And it's all dragged out, no holds barred. Kick . . . punch . . . scratch . . . spitting . . . screaming. Fight. And when it's over and the streets are soaking up the blood, you smile and know that you just won another day with yourself. He's trying to take the only real thing I dream of . . . the reason for my surviving. I live with the dream of seeing her smile at the sound of my name. I won't let him destroy that dream . . . I won't let him. Yeah, I'm going to kill me a pimp. (*Lights.*)

SCENE 2. *Out of freeze. Justice's bar. Chile is at piano singing. The scene is jumping.*

CHILE: OOOOOOOO la la la la la la la
Wake up on the morning and find
Your dreams behind
Every kind of rainbow in every color scheme.
It's the players golden rule . . .
That the sun always shines for the cool.

(*Chorus*)

OOOOOOOO la la la la la la la
So wear your eternal high
As you hustle to get by
Sport your fancy clothes
And let the whole world know
That you belong to that school
Where the sun always shines . . . for the cool.

OOOOOOOO la la la la la la la
But when the neon lights are dark,
That's when you shed your player's heart
Being free to fall in love with me.
Until then I'll remember, the players golden rule
That the sun always shines for the cool . . .

33

OOOOOOOO la la la la
Remember the player's golden rule
That the sun always shines . . . for the cool.

Thank you . . . thank you.

DIAMOND: Go, Chile girl, with your bad self . . . walk on girl. Girl
. . . man, that girl does harder than a broke dick dog. Oh shit,
you know . . . there is too much sunlight in here . . . let me fish
out my shades. As they say in the old mack game, the suns always
shines for the cool.

WILLIE BODEGA: Hey, Diamond!

DIAMOND: Yeah, Willie . . . Yeah, man, be cool . . .

WILLIE BODEGA: The drinks are on Diamond Ring, so drink,
sing, dance and be merry . . .

DIAMOND: Wait a second, Willie, I never said anything about
buying the whole house a drink.

WILLIE BODEGA: What, man? I just asked you and you said,
"Yeah, Willie, yeah, Willie, be cool."

DIAMOND: Shit, man, I didn't know what the fuck you were
talking about, man. You a jive motherfucker. You sure there
wasn't a nigger in your family somewhere? Cuz you about the
niggerest nigger I know, and you ain't even black.

WILLIE BODEGA: Do I take that as a compliment or an insult?

DIAMOND: (To Jr.) I told the whole place how jive this whitey is
and no one listened.

WILLIE BODEGA: That's cuz you was lying.

DIAMOND: Diamond Ring never lies.

CAT EYES: That is a fucking lie.

DIAMOND: Man, I don't remember asking you for a comment.

CAT EYES: Well, you got one . . . so what. (Diamond lifts hat and
Kahlu crosses to other women gathered near lounge.)

DIAMOND: Man, when I was a kid and I wasn't wanted around . . . I
knew. Some people you can't hint them away because of their
hard face. You know what I mean, man?

JR. BALLOON: He must be from Vajado . . . el pueblo de los cara
duro.

CAT EYES: I'm from la Perla, pa'que te lo coma', con leche, cabrón.

JR. BALLOON: Vete a coger por culo mamao.

CAT EYES: Oye, lo tuyo viene por ahí.

JR. BALLOON: Hey, did you guys hear what jumped down with Tito Pan Doblao?

WILLIE BODEGA: Tito Fold Bread?

JR. BALLOON: Yeah, man, you know the heist kid from out of the East Side.

WILLIE BODEGA: Oh yeah, yeah . . . I remember him. How you gonna forget a dude named Fold Bread?

JR. BALLOON: Man, I don't know what get into people sometimes, tú sabé? Pero, like, this dude has a good thing going with himself. Tú sabé, like he was out here making a good dollar doing the simple shit he does . . . tú sabé? . . . like this dude was on parole man, ten years on the motherfucking paper. Dig? And el chamaco goes out and does his thing, fronting a job in a store he practically owned. Tú sabé . . . Hey, Bam-Bam, when did you tell me about Pan Doblao?

BAM-BAM: Friday . . . I got the news clipping. You wanna see it?

JR. BALLOON: Yeah man, let me have it.

BAM-BAM: I sell it to you for a dollar.

JR. BALLOON: Man, dig this motherfucker here.

WILLIE BODEGA: Hey man . . . I'll buy it.

JR. BALLOON: He a sucker for kids.

WILLIE BODEGA: Anyone that tries to sell you a newspaper clipping got to really be out here hustling his motherfucking ass off . . .yeah man, you got to give it to him. He tries harder than Satan.

BAM-BAM: That's cuz I'm god's nephew, Willie.

JR. BALLOON: Go on kid, tell him how much of a sucker he is. He don't know nothing. Right kid?

BAM-BAM: Willie knows a whole lot. He even teaches me math in his house. (Cross to Viva at piano.)

JR. BALLOON: You do Willie?

DIAMOND: Not bad, Willie B.

WILLIE BODEGA: Yeah, so what? So I know a little bit of math.

JR. BALLOON: Nothing, tú sabé, just asking.

SATISFACTION: Hell, don't remember the very first one. Well, I remember the first trick I turned. Guess who. My elementary school principal. Really . . . this one is something else . . . I was about eleven . . .

CHILE: Eleven!

SATISFACTION: No . . . seriously, I was taking a smoke in the girls' bathroom . . . no, not marijuana . . . tobacco, just plain tobacco.

Well, school was out and I didn't hear the bell ring . . . so there I was, by myself, in the john, smoking a cigarette and Mr. Sanders, that was his name . . . never can forget it. . . . Anyway, he comes in and stands there looking at me. Now, at the time I was sleeping with my brother . . . no, not fucking, just sleeping . . . and in the morning he would get up and try to cover his "thing" but I could always see that it was hard . . . I found out later that most guys wake in the morning with it hard . . . anyway he caught me smoking, right . . . you now, an infraction . . . so he starts giving me this lecture and I pretend to be sorry and all ears to everything he's saying. So he puts his hand on my shoulder, right, comforting me and all that shit. But I see this bulge in his pants. Now, like I told you, I slept with my little brother and he use' to have this friend that would take him to school in the morning and I would pretend I was sleeping and he would feel me and jerk off all fast kind of business . . .

PHEBE: You sure take a long time to get where you're going. Tell me about the principal.

SATISFACTION: Oh, yeah . . . him . . . well, anyway, my brother's friend used to always say, if I ever wanted to make a little money, just let him know and he would give me the whole wallet . . .

PHEBE: I bet he would.

SATISFACTION: So, the first thing that come into my head, while Mr. Sanders was feeling me, was to ask for a dollar. So, he pulled out his wallet and gives me a twenty . . . pulls me into the toilet stall . . . and he's a big guy and I'm kinda small . . .

CHILE: Kinda?

SATISFACTION: Well, I'm not a midget. This was really freaky here. We are in this small space . . . oh well, then he pulls it out and I let out with a WOW Mr. Sanders and he starts shushing me quiet, "please, we'll get caught." Man, it was big and fat.

CHILE: Spare me.

SATISFACTION: Well, you asked. He couldn't fit the place, right, and for the both of us it was tight. He sat on the bowl and let out this big fart . . . man it stunk. (*Cross Kahlu to bar.*) . . . We're all in these weird positions trying to settle on the right angle. Anyway, nothing works and he gets really pissed off . . . he takes me by the neck, pulls me down to my knees and tries to put it in my mouth . . . but you know I wasn't into that and that's where the money is, you know? Anyway, he came in my hair and shits on himself . . . (*Cross Kahlu from bar, turns and goes back.*) and

I'm thinking he's catching a heart attack, and all he kept saying was, "cold water . . . cold water . . . put cold water on your hair." Anyway, they found him the next morning with a hard-on . . . but dead.

PHEBE: Chile, did you ever turn someone? Did you ever?

SATISFACTION: Naw, she still a virgin . . . at her age too . . . ridiculous . . . really, girl, sex is sound of mind . . .

CHILE: I am not a virgin.

SATISFACTION: I'm shocked.

PHEBE: I think I'm gonna faint . . . hold me somebody . . .

CHILE: Well, my name isn't Mary of Nazareth . . . it's Chile Girl . . .

(Diamond and Junior enter from lounge.)

DIAMOND: Oh shit, man, he got busted for that? Wow, like why would he do some dumb shit like that. Wow, that's some strange shit ain't it?

WILLIE BODEGA: Weird, man, weird, all kinds of weird people in this world.

JR. BALLOON: Like the dude had all this thing going for him, tú sabé, and a couple of women that were put on him, tú sabé. What would make a dude that got all this shit going for him go out, pull a robbery and then rape the bitch too? . . . I mean he was asking to get taken off the count the way I see it, tú sabé . . .

CHILE: Bam-Bam Boy, come here. Listen, go to the kitchen and get Lefty some shot glasses.

BAM-BAM: Momentito . . . oye, Willie . . . let me have my money.

WILLIE BODEGA: Here, I don't want it . . .

BAM-BAM: Cuz you already read it.

WILLIE BODEGA: That's right, son . . . like anytime you got something to sell, never let the person you selling it to get a hold of it without el dinero en su mano. You know money talks.

BAM-BAM: Bullshit walks . . .

WILLIE BODEGA: Start walkin'.

JR. BALLOON: That's part of your math lesson from the Street University.

CHILE: Go on, hurry . . . we need the glasses fast, Bam-Bam . . .He cute, ain't he?

WILLIE BODEGA: If that type turn you on, I guess so. He's not my type, you know.

CHILE: Go hump yourself . . .

WILLIE BODEGA: I will, thank you, Chile Girl.

JR. BALLOON: But I tell you, man, tú sabé, that shit with Pan

Doblao is really fucking too much, man, too strong.

WILLIE BODEGA: Yeah, I never expect him to come out of a bag like that, like that don't sound like him at all. Right?

DIAMOND: Man, you never know anything about anybody until the shit comes out in the wash. You know what I mean?

WILLIE BODEGA: Yeah, all of it comes out in the wash, man, all of it . . .

JR. BALLOON: Man, that old man should have been back by now . . . two hours with the girl.

WILLIE BODEGA: What you expect, man? He got a collar on him.

DIAMOND: Yeah, man, he got a collar on him.

JR. BALLOON: Why don't your woman talk, man?

WILLIE BODEGA: She's a mute, my man. She can't do that thing with the tongue.

DIAMOND: Man, the collar loosen up now. Hey, Viejo?

JR. BALLOON: Man, look like you lost some weight up there, Viejo.

VIEJO: In the joint?

JR. BALLOON: I ain't talking about no joint, motherfucker.

VIEJO: You can't be talking about nothing else.

JR. BALLOON: 'Pérate. She did take care of business with you. Right?

VIEJO: Oh, that. Yeah man, she took care of business . . . thanks for looking out . . .

JR. BALLOON: That's what friends are for. Ain't it? Shit, I don't need me no friends when I am doing good. Right, bro? Hey, man. Qué pasa with that dude with the pure shit? That dude having a wack attack and that's for real neal. He is supposed to have somthing nice for us tonight and like he ain't showed up yet, man. Tú sabé, me . . . I feel a little shakey around a dude that ain't got no sense of time.

WILLIE BODEGA: He be here, man, he be here. He might of had a flat tire. He might of got shot. Something!

DIAMOND: The only other whitey that I knew that had a sense of time beside you, Willie, was your brother, Billy Boy.

JR. BALLOON: Yeah, he was a good man . . .

VIEJO: Hey, man, Willie, I forgot to run it on you earlier, but like, I'm sorry to have heard about your brother man . . .

WILLIE BODEGA: Yeah, thanks a lot Viejo . . . you know he thought a great deal about you, man. He dug you a whole lot . . .

VIEJO: I dug on him too . . .

38

WILLIE BODEGA: Yeah . . .

VIEJO: Was you there when the shit jumped off?

WILLIE BODEGA: Yeah man, I was there, but there was nothing
that I could have done, man. You know, like he gave me the out,
man. He would've been really sore at me if I would have fucked
around and blew it. You know how Billy was, man. Let me tell
you something, Viejo. I'm sorry he dead, dig, but I'm proud at
the way he went, man, real proud at the way he went. Like that's
the way we should all go when the time comes that we have to say
it's a game of cards . . . holding court in the streets . . . guns
smoking, man, that's the way to do it when you got to do it.
Becuz when you play it that way, and you don't want to end the
game that way, then you should never had played anyway, right?
. . . Right! Like, that what's it all about, ain't it, man? Going
with your head held high and your trigger fingers aching . . .
man. Viejo, you know that I would have stayed with him if he
wanted me to. I would have gone with him to shake hands with
Satan. Shit, I bet he lonely down there . . . get all the heat . . .
man that's what he always got a lot of, fucking heat. Ever since I
could remember, man, our old man played it to the bitter end
with us. He played it so tough that we never learn what it meant
to be a little warm inside ourselves. But man, the time were like
hard candy in a cheap soda shop. But like that day, man, like that
day, I should have remember, "When a crosseyed mark gets in
your way, don't play," cuz it's bad luck . . . when you speak like
you ain't ever gonna see daylight again, man, that's the time to
spend in bed with pussy smelling pillows in your face. You know
that the time to hit the invisible man in the life scene, man, but
he knew all that too . . . he knew all that too, but he went
anyway, man. Viejo, he knew that too. You taught both of us
that shit way back then. You remember, right? . . . the roof top,
shootin' coke bottles off the edge. Man I was mean with a pistol
and so was he . . . but that day he spoke like he wasn't gonna
enjoy the bread from the sting no matter how much it was. It was
like he knew that there was a jinx in the air for him that day, but
he went. He insisted in making the hit anyway . . . it was like he
had what you call a bad ju ju, there was like no wind in the air . . .
man, no taste in our mouth, no feeling in our pulse, no beating in
our hearts, man. The train didn't even make noise for us that
day. The lights were all red in every corner that we came to, but
he wanted to go to the hit anyway . . . He was going for broke,

man. He was tired, I guess, like so many of us get tired with this whole thing out here. Remember the way he held his guns in his holsters, real close to his heart, man? But that day he held them down around his waist like if he wanted to put his head and heart out there for the buzzard in blue. He wanted to die, man. Viejo, he wanted to die and I didn't want him to . . . but like that his right to go if he wanted to. I see him running, man. He was running. The first cap was booked into his leg, man. He fell, got up and booked a cap into the man . . . they came out of nowhere, man. They came out of nowhere blasting them 38's his way. He was next to the building. They blew right through the door, and he came out as they walked his way where he was suppose to have been laying dead. He came out blasting caps into their asses, man. They ran, they ran and those that didn't lay down and play dead on the streets, were laid down dead. They laid down and played dead and I laugh cuz I knew that he was badder than all of them in the shining blue uniforms looking like semi-gods. He was a rebel. He was Satan in heaven fighting God for a piece of the action man. That's who he was, Lucifer, fighting God for a piece of the action. That's what he looked like. He looked like a young god taking his anger out on the fucking world. And he was mean-looking in his walk, in the bullets that flew out of his power. That was his power. That's why they had to kill him three times over after he was dead . .. but they should have known, man, that he was alive . . . he was more alive than they will ever be, cuz he was a rebel in the middle of them all, and he would have never hanged up his gloves . . . they were on his mitts for good and he wore them tight . . .

DIAMOND: Right. Solid on the wallet . . .

WILLIE BODEGA: Solid on the wallet? What kinda shit is that?

DIAMOND: Regular shit, my man, just plain ordinary shit.

WILLIE BODEGA: Sounds like it too . . .

JR. BALLOON: Oye, cut that shit out, man. You guys are beginning to bore me today with all this wolf-ticket selling that's going on around here. Shit, I feel like I'm at the arena and not in Justice's joint having a good time with the folks. Viva, play me a tune.

WILLIE BODEGA: Guess that kid Cat Eyes got me on edge all day, selling me a ticket, man. I should have cashed it for him, but man it's not worth it. He be out of the life a lot earlier than I thought he be . . .

DIAMOND: Yeah, he got on my nerves today too . . .

JR. BALLOON: Squash that shit too man . . . forget about that nonplayer . . .

WILLIE BODEGA: Viva, play me a little "Misty."

JR. BALLOON: Viejo, the kid's all right, you now . . . it's just that sometimes he comes across like bad medicine . . . like a laxative. You know what I mean? Tú sabé?

VIEJO: Yo sé . . . later . . . Lefty, rum and coke . . . easy on the coke. . . . What can I get you, Cat Eyes?

CAT EYES: Me? You gonna buy me a drink?

VIEJO: Yeah, why not? The enemies of two armies were at one time sitting together in the same room talking about which is the best way in which to kill men in wars . . .

CAT EYES: Freaky kind of shit. Ain't it?

VIEJO: Yeah, I guess some people would look at that as freaky, weird . . .fucked up thinking. But, you know, after they made up the rules they went out and had themselves a great big war to test out the rules and see which of them play fair . . .

CAT EYES: Who played fair?

VIEJO: Nobody ever plays fair when it involves the heart or the pocketbook . . .

CAT EYES: Look, old man, you kind of old to be talking like you mean to do something to somebody, you know, like the thing you said about your daughter . . . if she is your daughter.

VIEJO: She is my daughter . . call her . . . ask her . . .

CAT EYES: Chile Girl . . . here Cat Eyes . . .

CHILE: Yeah, what can I get you?

CAT EYES: Some questions answered . . .

CHILE: Like what?

CAT EYES: Like this man said that he's your father. Is that true?

VIEJO: You can deny it if you wish, niña, pero tú sabé en tu corazón que lo que pasó, pasó. Don't hold the world of yesterday against me, niña.

CHILE: He's the man that fucked my mother and created a child who he named Chile Girl Rivera. Yeah, if that's being a father, I guess he my father. Then it means nothing to me at all.

CHILE: Vaya, I guess that you want to say something to me on your own that ain't got her approval.

VIEJO: Her approval isn't needed in this case, young blood.

CHILE: Are you two discussing me and my life . . .

CAT EYES: Seems that your old man doesn't approve of me going out with you . . .

CHILE: It's no business of his, whatsoever.

CAT EYES: He thinks I am going to turn you out.

CHILE: That's because he sees himself in you, but you're different than he ever was with my mother. At least you can tell me the truth . . . even if it's in the dark. (*Cat Eyes kisses Chile.*)

VIEJO: You have a beautiful smile, Cat Eyes . . . you have the smile of a man that just got over like a fat rat . . . (*Shoves him.*)

CAT EYES: Hey, man. What the hell you doing? Get off my dick. Are you a faggot or something?

CHILE: What are you doing?

VIEJO: Punk, I got a 357 Magnum eight inch barrel sticking in your balls and if you don't be cool I'll blow them off.

CAT EYES: Man, be cool with that thing, man, but cool, please.

CHILE: Are you crazy? Haven't you done enough to me?

VIEJO: That's just it, I have done too much to you and I never have done anything for you. Now I'll make it up to you, tonight, baby . . . tonight . . . right here.

CHILE: By killing my man?

CAT EYES: Talk to him, baby. He looks crazy, man . . . he looks crazy. Talk to him, baby, talk to him. Please, Viejo, man, shoot anywhere else but there, please man.

VIEJO: Chile, I ain't out to kill your man but to kill your would-be pimp.

CAT EYES: Man, I ain't her pimp, man, I love her. Believe me, I do.

VIEJO: You lying punk son of a bitch . . . get up . . . up . . . faggot up . . . get your yellow ass up in the air. Get it up, punk. (*Diamond crosses from dance floor.*)

DIAMOND: Oh shit. What the fuck is Viejo doing. (*Everyone gathers around.*)

WILLIE BODEGA: Oh shit, he gonna kill that kid . . . Viejo.

VIEJO: Shut up, all of you . . . keep out of it . . .

WILLIE BODEGA: Man, you just got out . . . if you wanna waste him let me take care of it. That's my shot, man, not yours . . .

JUSTICE: Viejo . . . don't . . .

CAT EYES: Please don't kill me, please . . . don't kill me.

VIEJO: Punk, I ain't going to kill you, but you gonna wish that I had.

JUSTICE: Viejo, man, you gone crazy, man? What are you trying to prove, man? He's a punk kid, man, just a punk kid.

VIEJO: Is he right? You ain't nothing but a punk kid? They fucked you in the joint . . . is that what he is saying? Answer me.

CAT EYES: Yeah, man, I ain't nothing but a punk kid.

42

VIEJO: You gave it up in the joint. Didn't you?

CAT EYES: Yeah, man, I gave up my ass in the joint . . .

ROSA: Carlos, please do what he says . . . he's crazy.

CAT EYES: Man, what have I done to you? Man, I ain't done nothing to you, man, nothing . . . I don't even know you.

VIEJO: But you know my daughter. Don't you, motherfucker? And you wanna turn her out. Don't you? That's what you told me. Didn't you?

CAT EYES: Yeah, man, but I didn't mean it.

CHILE: Did you say that?

CAT EYES: Yeah, baby, but I was only kidding, baby, believe me.

VIEJO: Liar!

CAT EYES: Okay . . . okay . . . I did mean it . . . but man, let me go and I won't even look at her anymore. I mean it, man, really.

VIEJO: Why should I believe you, man? You lied to her . . . you lied to me . . . you lied to everybody, you bullshiting punk.

CAT EYES: No, Viejo, not this time. I swear on my mother's grave.

VIEJO: Rosa . . . Rosa, tell Chile what you are to this thing here?

ROSA: I . . . I . . .

CAT EYES: Rosa, Rosa . . . cállate, te corto tu cuello. Rosa . . .

VIEJO: Shut the fuck up, faggot. Go on, Rosa, tell her.

ROSA: He's my brother . . .

VIEJO: See, baby? I know punks like him, I know them all my life. . . . You love him and you don't believe . . . but it's the truth, baby, the truth . . . he put his own sister out on the corner to hustle. He sold her to Junior Balloon.

ROSA: We had to survive . . .

VIEJO: There are other ways to make it out here, in any of the games of the fast . . .

WILLIE BODEGA: Man, he started out on his own family, man, that's out . . .

DIAMOND: He needs to die.

CHILE: No man needs to die.

VIEJO: Baby, this is one scumbag that needs to die.

CAT EYES: I don't wanna die, man, please don't do it . . . take pity.

CHILE: Shut up! Die if you have to, but don't beg for pity.

CAT EYES: Fuck you, you ain't the one that gonna get wasted.

VIEJO: I ain't gonna waste you . . . you gonna do it yourself. You got to go slow man, you got to know your mistake everyday that you are gonna live . . .

CHILE: Punk . . . Punk . . .

JUSTICE: Stay right where you are, Chile . . . stay right where you are.

VIEJO: Strip, punk!

DIAMOND: Sissy ass motherfucker had the heart to sell tickets . . . shit . . .

JR. BALLOON: Shut up, Diamond

DIAMOND: Fuck you.

WILLIE BODEGA: Lefty . . . cool this will you . . .

LEFTY G.: No, man, you guys cool it. (*Pulls gun.*)

VIEJO: Get down on your knees, punk . . . down on your knees.

PHEBE: Cat Eyes . . . baby . . . don't . . . baby . . .

DIAMOND: You're mine now bitch . . . so get over here and enjoy the show. . . . Move!

VIEJO: Get down on your knees, faggot . . .

WILLIE BODEGA: Get down on your knees, man . . .

JR. BALLOON: Get down on your knees, maricón.

CAT EYES: Man, be cool, please be cool . . . I getting down.

VIEJO: On your knees, mariconcito . . . down . . .

CHILE: Cat Eyes . . .

JUSTICE: Get down, boy, if you wanna live . . .

VIEJO: Now beg . . . motherfucker, beg . . . (*Lefty locks door.*) like you wanna live. I want you to beg me like if you wanna stay alive as bad as you wanna live, that's as bad as I wanna hear you beg. Am I God?

CHILE: No, papi, no . . . no, Carlos . . .

CAT EYES: Yes, you are God . . .

VIEJO: I see there are tears in your eyes . . . cry motherfucker, cry . . . scream out . . . scream out your tears, motherfucker, scream them out, you no-good-low-life son of a whore. (*Cat Eyes begins to scream and cry. He holds on to Viejo's legs.*) Kiss my shoes punk, kiss them. (*Cat Eyes complies with all of Viejo's wishes.*) Everybody back, back, every motherfucking body get your ass away from here . . . move you son of a bitch, move.

JUSTICE: Viejo . . . Viejo . . .

VIEJO: You too, you ugly motherfucker, move back . . . stop crying already, you would-be king of the pimps. You a player? You couldn't play a dime off a blind man in a dark alley. Sucker, you ain't never played where the action is you and you alone . . . because on the street the game is staying alive and you don't know how to stay alive . . . you don't know how to survive because you put yourself in a position to die. . . . Like right now,

44

sucker, you are going to die, Cat Eyes, the pimp . . . Cat Eyes the pussy . . . you a player? A player is a survivor of a constant struggle to do it hard . . . to play it to the bitter end. . . . Faggot, don't you know that out here in this jungle if you are caught acting, you are one dead player? Out here you go for broke . . . you take it to the streets on all levels and you took it to the level that's gonna cause your death. This ain't the semi-truth world of the tennis hustler or the pro golf pusher, this is the real world of the dreamer strung out. But you can't understand that. Are you listening, Chile Girl? He ain't shit. He's a phony being, a fake . . . even his lies are false. You blew this the minute that you thought you were the only player in town that made the rules. I invented the game. You can't hustle off a hustler. You can't play on a player. You gave yourself no out. You put yourself in solitary confinement, baby. They tell me if you don't open your mouth when you are dying, you don't need any questions answered about death. Motherfucker, I told you and you closed your ears; now you close your life. I won't let you get away with it, not me. I won't let you, motherfucker . . .

CHILE: No, no lo mate, papi, no tire . . .

JUSTICE: Viejo . . . *Viejo shoots himself and goes to the bar. At sound of shot Cat Eyes falls back searching for a wound, crying and screaming for Chile. Everyone rushes to Cat Eyes thinking he is shot.)*

DIAMOND: You ain't shot . . . he ain't shot, man, look, he ain't shot.

WILLIE BODEGA: Oh, shit, Viejo played it . . . it was his play and he played it.

JR. BALLOON: The motherfucker was a blank . . . *(Kahlu screams, Viejo falls . . . dead.)*

JUSTICE: Girl, what's the matter with you? Viejo!

CHILE: No, papi . . . no! *(Rushes to Viejo.)*

JUSTICE: He played it . . . to the bitter end. *(The cast exits two or three at a time. Willie is the last to exit, leaving Viejo, Cat Eyes and Chile.)*

A Midnight Moon at the Greasy Spoon

CHARACTERS

Joseph Scott, *Late sixties, active, strong.*
Gerald Fisher, *Late sixties, active, strong.*
Dominick Skorpios, *Late thirties, Greek immigrant.*
Fred Pulley, *Early seventies.*
Night-Life, *Mid twenties.*
Joe the Cop, *Late fifties.*
Zulma Samson, *Late forties.*
Jake the Nigger, *Late forties.*
Reynolds, *FBI Man.*
Lockhart, *Bureau of Immigration.*
Man One, *Insurance Salesman.*
Man Two, *Record Company Executive.*
Hooker One, *On a string.*
Hooker Two, *Freelancer.*
Shopping Bag Lady, *Mumbles.*
Junkie Girl, *Far gone.*
Lost Man, *From out of town.*
Boy, *Songwriter, musician.*
Girl, *Singer.*

Plus as many miscellaneous customers as can be creatively accommodated.

ACT I

A small luncheonette in the Times Square area servicing the workers of the New York Times and whatever hungry people come in to eat. The place is open all night. In half light frozen like the figures in Edward Hopper's "Night Hawk," Gerry is at the coffee urn, Dominick prepares to cut the pie, Joe is poised at the cash register preparing to make change for a departing Customer, Hooker One is on the pay phone, A Biker sits at the counter waiting for his coffee, a Student sits at a side counter reading a textbook. After a moment the lights go to full and the action begins. General ad libs as Gerry serves the Biker, the Customer pays Joe, Dominick serves a piece of pie to the Student. Then . . .

DOMINICK: There's not enough pies to last the night, Joe.

JOE: So what.

GERRY: So what? So what, he says, like if he don't like making money.

JOE: Listen, you were supposed to order the pies, right?

DOMINICK: I told you yesterday that I couldn't order the pies 'cause I was coming in late today . . .

JOE: You came in on time.

DOMINICK: Well the marriage was faster than I thought it was going to be like.

GERRY: Welcome to America, Dominick.

JOE: How was the wedding, Dominick?

DOMINICK: Very fast . . . very fast . . . I go into the place in the morning, we sign some papers, we go into a room . . . One, two, three, that's it. I bring my cousin Aristotle with us as a best man. She had some junkie girl with her as best woman.

JOE: Maid of honor.

DOMINICK: What honor, Joe . . . she had no honor, bring a girl like that to her wedding. She's crazy without honor, thank God I'm not going to live with her.

JOE: What do you mean you're not gonna live with her?

DOMINICK: You know why I married her.

JOE: Sure I know, but you got to get between them legs of hers at least once.

GERRY: Yeah, Dominick, after all the money you put out for her to marry you, you got to get laid at least once to make it legal, you know what I mean Dominick?

DOMINICK: Sure I know what you mean, but this is strictly busi-

47

ness.

JOE: It may be strictly business, Dom, but anytime you can get a piece of leg that looks like a piece of leg you ought to get that piece of leg before she gets away . . . you know what I mean, Dominick.

DOMINICK: I don't know.

JOE: What do you mean, you don't know?

GERRY: She's your wife, you got a right to get a piece of leg.

DOMINICK: But this is strictly business . . .

JOE: Anytime, anywhere in America a man is the boss of his home. Your wife is bought and paid for, she's yours, Dominick.

DOMINICK: I don't know . . .

GERRY: What's there to know, all you got to do when she comes home . . .

DOMINICK: She ain't coming home.

JOE: You mean she isn't coming home . . .? She's got to come home.

GERRY: Where else is a wife supposed to go but home?

DOMINICK: I mean there is no home to come home to.

GERRY: No home to come home to. That doesn't even sound right.

JOE: That's a great title for a song. (*Singing.*) There's no home to come home to, like no home that I know. What's a home without a piece of leg.

DOMINICK: Look, after the wedding she went her way, I came here.

GERRY: Ain't you gonna see her again?

DOMINICK: When the divorce papers come through.

JOE: But that's not gonna be for a long time.

GERRY: Yeah, that's right, and besides, you have to become a citizen first before you divorce her. Don't forget that.

JOE: Don't be stupid, Gerry, that's why he married her.

GERRY: I know why he married her . . .

DOMINICK: Joe, what if she doesn't . . .

JOE: She has no choice.

DOMINICK: . . . she can say, go fuck your own leg instead.

JOE: Don't be stupid, Dominick, she can't say that.

GERRY: Why not?

DOMINICK: Yeah, why not?

JOE: Because she can't say that.

GERRY: That doesn't make any sense to me.

DOMINICK: To me either, it makes no sense to me.

48

JOE: Why does everything have to make sense?

GERRY: Joe, if things don't make any sense, then you can't execute them.

JOE: Hey, Gerry, give me that cloth there.

GERRY: Catch.

JOE: No . . . oh shit, look at this. You got the thing inside the chocolate syrup, dummy.

GERRY: Here . . .

DOMINICK: What happened with what you were saying, Joe?

JOE: I'm thinking Dominick, let me think.

GERRY: You want maybe we should go outside in case you blow a fuse?

JOE: Oh, oh, oh . . . Dominick, how much you laid out to marry that broad?

DOMINICK: Close to three thousand dollars.

GERRY: That's a lot of money to become a citizen of the USA.

JOE: Yeah, with so many people trying to get out of the USA.

GERRY: As far as I'm concerned, I still go with the good old saying . . . love it or leave it. If you don't like it, get your ass out.

JOE: Boy, if people knew that people like Dominick work for years to save up enough money so that they can marry some broad and become a citizen . . .

GERRY: What are you doing, Joe? Campaigning for mayor?

JOE: I bet if I did campaign for mayor I'd win by a landslide, 'cause I know what this town needs, somebody strong that's not afraid to kick some ass in that mansion, who's not afraid of the mafia or the union bosses or doesn't have his hand out for kickbacks all the time. You know that's what this town needs. If I was mayor, the schools wouldn't be full of drugs and police and revolutionaries. I'd put them all up against the wall and shoot 'em, no trials. I'd arrest them and shoot them on the spot like Castro did in Cuba.

GERRY: How do you know what Castro did in Cuba?

JOE: Because that's what all them Communists do when they take over. They have a blood bath to clean out all the people that gave them a bad time.

GERRY: You sound like a communist.

JOE: I don't sound like a communist. Don't say things like that. You know the walls have ears. This place may be tapped.

DOMINICK: Hey Joe, have you thought about? . . .

JOE: What?

DOMINICK: What we were talking about.

JOE: I haven't thought of nothing as yet but I will. Just let the old noggin get to work and we'll have a brain storm.

GERRY: Yeah, maybe we should get an umbrella, hey.

JOE: Maybe we should get an umbrella. That's funny, real funny. You know the communists don't have a bad idea when they start out, you know. I mean it. I mean like they have a good idea when they start to throw out the rotten apple before it contaminates the whole barrel. That's their motto and like it or not, it's a good one. If we had in this country stopped all them spicks and niggers from going crazy protesting this and that, we would have been in a better more orderly country. We let all the foreigners come in and tell us what to do with our country. Ridiculous. That's why this country is falling apart now, you know that. Why I read in the *Daily News* yesterday that one of the top men in the Mayor's administration was arrested for being a crook. And look what happened to Kennedy and his brother. The poor kid didn't have a chance to get anywhere.

GERRY: You think he had a chance at being the President?

JOE: Are you kidding! With all the money his family has!

GERRY: Them Kennedys sure have had a bad time with their kids. All of them killed and running around, never being at home. Sure is hell of a family life they have, huh?

JOE: Now Joe Kennedy was one hell of a man. Let me tell you he was a real old timer. He was one of them old time pioneers.

DOMINICK: You mean he was with Wyatt Earp and Billy the Kid?

JOE: Naw, well, I bet he might have known them. I mean he had the guts to know them.

GERRY: He didn't know them.

JOE: What do you know! You know anything of the Kennedy family.

GERRY: No.

JOE: Well, I'm an expert on the Kennedy family. I know everything about them. I didn't vote for John because he was too young and wouldn't know how to handle a country the size of this one. If he had been running for Governor or Senator or maybe Mayor of the City, I might have voted for him. But for president, naw. I mean he was killed just in time.

GERRY: What a crazy thing to say, that the president was killed just in time.

JOE: What I mean is if he had lived, everybody would have seen how lousy a president this man was and he would have never gotten the chance to run for any office again.

DOMINICK: But Joe, he must have been a great president. I mean when I came here, I landed in Kennedy Airport. I read of a place that they call Cape Kennedy where they shot those rockets to the moon. I mean, that to me means that he was a great man.

JOE: Who's saying he wasn't a great man? He got killed didn't he?

GERRY: So what does that prove?

JOE: It proves that he was a great man. All great men get assassinated, right? What was the name of the colored guy that got killed in the south, you know, the guy who walked all over the place?

GERRY: King.

JOE: What?

GERRY: That was his name, King. They got some kind of center down here named after him, he said that . . .

JOE: Said what?

GERRY: That little black boys and little white boys would be holding hands.

JOE: If I caught my son skipping down the streets holding hands with some nigger boy, I'd break his arm.

GERRY: I don't care if he's black or white or yellow or red, if I caught my son holding another boy's hand, I'd do the same thing too. No son of mine is gonna hold any man's hand and skip down the street like some freakin' fairy.

DOMINICK: "I have a dream."

JOE: You have a dream?

DOMINICK: That was the thing he said.

JOE: Who said?

DOMINICK: Doctor Martin Luther King, Jr.

JOE: Who's that?

GERRY: That's the name of the guy who made the speech we were just talking about.

JOE: How do you know his name, Gerry? How'd you know his name, Dominick.

DOMINICK: I read about him in school. He was really a beautiful human being.

JOE: What do you know? Look, you're a foreigner here. . . . What do you know about the niggers in this country? Them spades can really turn on you. They have no manners. I had a spook working here a couple of years ago and he was really a nasty-mouth nigger. I mean he would cough in front of people who sat down to eat. He'd pick his nose in public, farted all the time and then would stink like a dead cat stinks. I think his stomach was rotten or something, you know. Everytime he went downstairs to the basement to shit, the smell would just fill this whole place.

GERRY: Joe please, I'm eating.

JOE: So go ahead and eat, who's stopping you?

GERRY: Never mind.

JOE: I had to let him go. After that I had a spick working in here and I had to keep my eye on him all the time. You know you can't trust a spick. They steal everything that's not nailed to the floor. I mean, he was a good worker, but like, I had to keep my eye on him all the time, you know.

DOMINICK: Did he steal?

GERRY: Who knows? But Joe's right; them spicks steal like if, you know what it is being a thief comes to them natural, like making money comes to us. It's a second nature to them.

DOMINICK: Did you see him steal anything?

JOE: That's what Gerry is saying. They are just like the Arab. They can steal the nails off Jesus Christ and still leave him hanging on the cross. I had a spick friend of mine who once told me that at an early age their parents teach them how to steal and lie and everything. It's like going to school I mean.

DOMINICK: Did you believe him?

JOE: Of course I believed him. He wouldn't lie to me.

DOMINICK: I don't know, Joe. Like this country is full of all different kinds of people, you know.

JOE: I know, I know, ain't that a fact, but that's because we're kind. We let all kinds of people in this country of ours. We're not selfish with our wealth. With the opportunities that are here for all people, what the hell.

GERRY: Yeah, you know the old saying, you can't keep it unless you give it away.

JOE: What'd you say, Gerry?

GERRY: You know, it's better to give than receive . . . or like them holy rollers tell you . . . can't get into heaven with all that money so give it to me? Like Holly Nel said, a camel can't pass anything if you put a needle in his eye. (*Gerry exits to back.*)

FRED: (*Entering.*) Hey, where's the bum?

JOE: Hey bum, how are ya?

FRED: Okay, how ya doing, bum? Where's the other bum?

JOE: He's in the back. Hey, Gerry.

GERRY: Yeah?

JOE: Fred's out here . . .

GERRY: Hey, bum.

FRED: That's right, you bum, stay back there and rot, you bum.

GERRY: Ah, you don't wanna see me 'cause you owe me some money!

FRED: Where do I owe money to a bum from? Oh yeah, that's right. You were begging on the subways and I told you I'd have to owe you . . . for a cup of coffee.

JOE: That's a great one.

FRED: Hey, Dominick, how are ya doing?

DOMINICK: Okay, Fred.

FRED: The name is Mister Pulley.

DOMINICK: Okay, Mr. Pulley.

JOE: Ain't you got no manners for senior citizens?

DOMINICK: I do, I'm sorry sir.

FRED: That's quite all right. Just don't let it happen again.

DOMINICK: No sir, I won't.

FRED: (To Joe.) Did you get tickets for the roller derby this Saturday?

JOE: I'm gonna watch it on TV.

FRED: Watch it on TV? You must be getting old, you bum. To watch it out there in person is the way to see roller derby. Let me tell you there is nothing like it. When Mike Gannon goes around that turn knocking everything and everybody out of his way . . . Let me tell you something, you bum, that's a sight to see. There's nothing like it and you can't tell me you really get the whole thing on TV because I know, I've watched the roller derby on TV and it is not the same thing as watching it out there with that crowd yelling for blood. And you don't get to see what really goes on when them Amazons get it on in a fisticuff action. Them torn clothes reveals a lot more than they show on TV. Can you know what I mean? Some of them girls are really built like brick shithouses. Some of them broads remind me of the battleship I was stationed on during the big one.

JOE: Yeah, I know, but I gotta lotta work to do around the house, you know.

FRED: Let me get a cup of coffee and a toasted muffin.

JOE: Hey, Gerry, get the bum his regular.

GERRY: Okay, a toasted English coming up. (Dominick hands Joe a cup of coffee for Fred.)

FRED: Hey, Dominick, you feel like making a couple'a bucks this weekend?

DOMINICK: I don't know if I have time this weekend.

JOE: Dominick just got married today.

FRED: Hey, congratulations, Dominick.

JOE: *(Handing Fred the coffee.)* He married a Puerto Rican.

FRED: A what?

GERRY: *(Entering with the English muffin.)* You heard him.

FRED: Hey, bum!

GERRY: Hey, bum!

FRED: So you married a Puerto Rican girl, huh? I hear tell they are some hot little number.

GERRY: That's what I hear too. I mean I never had me one of those.

FRED: You probably get a heart attack if one of them little numbers got on you, you bum.

JOE: They would sure do a number on him.

FRED: They sure would, thanks. Where's the Sweet and Low?

GERRY: Here ya are, service with a smile.

FRED: Your smile I don't need, hey.

JOE: Hey Dominick, you wanna pass a mop on the floor before they start coming in here.

FRED: Yeah, so Dominick got himself hooked up to a little Puerto Rican number, huh? Hey, Dominick, you got more brains than I thought you had. By the way, how old are you?

GERRY: How old are you, Dominick?

DOMINICK: Thirty-eight years old next month.

FRED: You gonna stay in this country now, Dominick?

DOMINICK: Yes.

JOE: Sure he is, that's why he married that spick!

FRED: How she look?

JOE: She's a looker, that's for sure.

GERRY: Yeah, she sure is. Three thousand dollars worth of looks.

FRED: Three thousand dollars, are you kidding?

JOE: Nope, that's what he paid to marry her.

FRED: Hell, for three grand I would have married him.

GERRY: You're not exactly his type, Fred.

FRED: I could be just like Jack Lemmon in that film with Marilyn Monroe. What was the name of that movie? I saw it three times with Jack Lemmon, a real funny guy. I seen all his movies you know.

GERRY: "Some Like It Hot!" . . .

FRED: That's it, "Some Like It Hot," a great film.

JOE: They don't make films like that any more, you know.

FRED: That's a darn shame, isn't it?

GERRY: It sure is.

DOMINICK: Can I still see it in the movies?

FRED: The late, late, late movie.

JOE: Fred, you're a riot.

JOE THE COP: (Entering.) Hey, Joe, how's tricks?

JOE: Tricks are for kids, want some corn flakes?

JOE THE COP: Hello, Dominick.

DOMINICK: Hello, Officer Joe.

JOE: Dominick, get some glasses.

GERRY: What'll you have?

JOE THE COP: Give me a pastrami on white, hold the mustard. Coffee with no sugar.

GERRY: And an apple turnover, all traveling, right?

JOE THE COP: Right. So how's business?

JOE: Business is fine. How's business out there in the streets?

JOE THE COP: Same as always. Saturday night everybody is trying to kill somebody else.

JOE: Things get bad some times out there, right?

JOE THE COP: You're damn right. Especially on nights like this. The weather isn't so bad, it's a good night for muggers. People wanna go out and take walks. I wish people would just go home and lock themselves in until it's time to go to work the next day. That's what I do, well not me, Joe, but my wife and kids I mean. If my kids aren't home by eight o'clock, I go looking for them and when I find them they know what's in store for them. Most parents nowadays don't wanna hit their kids no matter what they do. If it was up to me every kid that came into the station house would receive an ass whipping like my father use to give me.

JOE: I know what you mean. My kids are all grown up now and all of them with the exception of the oldest are hard working citizens making their daily living. No charity crap for them. The oldest one went to Vietnam and came back a . . . a . . . I don't know what to call him . . . a communist junkie pinko fag creep. I threw the bum out of the house.

FRED: I fought in the big one and these kids go out to a little brawl like Vietnam and they make a big stink out of it. They really think they been to war. They come back talking life if they, they, they . . .

JOE: I know what you mean, Fred. I can't even begin to pinpoint the problem of the chicken-livered shithead.

JOE THE COP: Well, they finally gave me a desk job now.

JOE: You got yourself a desk job at the station?

JOE THE COP: Yep, taking it easy.

JOE: What are you two doing there with Dominick?

GERRY: Wouldn't you like to know.

FRED: Just trying to help the young fella along with some marital hints, you know what I mean?

JOE: Dominick just got married.

JOE THE COP: He did, huh? Dom old boy, you just made one of America's grave yet traditional human errors.

DOMINICK: I did? How?

JOE THE COP: Dropping the wings of bachelor freedom and donning the yoke of marriage slavery, but nevertheless, I wish you health, wealth and love . . .

JOE: I'll drink to that.

DOMINICK: Thank you . . . thank you very much . . . (*Enter Zulma in a rush*)

ZULMA: Hi, everybody . . . hot chocolate to go . . . extra milk . . . no sugar . . . is the phone working, Joe? My, Gerry, the years are taking their toll . . . potbelly, pretty soon. Stop drinking all that beer, right Fred? Hey, Dominick . . . hello . . . this is X-87 . . . nothing . . . What? No . . . but I will . . . well if that's the way you feel about it then okay. I'll just get me another answering service . . . goodbye . . . Chocolate ready? I was going to get me another service anyway . . . I was . . . really . . . oh well, Joe, you know how it is in the business, sometime you're up, sometimes you're down . . . but I guess I know what you're thinking once a person reaches a certain point in the struggle to reach some kind of notoriety and they don't get there then it's time to bid farewell to all that is a part of one's natural habit as is the habit to eat to breath to sleep. The nature of a prayer is to be heard by whoever is listening, I seem to have a bad connection to that certain ear wherever it is.

JOE: What are you talking about?

GERRY: Dominick here just got married.

JOE THE COP: Would you mind repeating what you just said, I didn't get it all.

ZULMA: What I'm talking about? I'm talking about David Merrick . . . Alex Cohan . . . Gower Champion . . . Joe Luggage and Frankie Suitcase, about all those guys who control the means and the manner of my existence on this planet, about *Show Business* and *Backstage* and *Variety* and all those casting notices that appear in the paper, about the Equity billboard, about the daydreams that rush through our heads as we climb the stairs to an audition, about the tears that flood out after being rejected once . . . twice . . . three times in one afternoon . . . and that's not counting the morning, or the telephone calls, the hundreds of pictures and résumés that hit the mailboxes . . . of course, I can't repeat what I said, I speak from the moment not from a script . . . as for you, Dominick who just got married, break a leg . . . well, time has it that I venture forth toward the unknown fate of a sacred audition . . . this hot chocolate will be cold by the time I reach my destination, but that's not the moment of truth . . . it comes later on in the day with the hot chicken soup that I heat in the naked cold of my lonely room . . . when the night finds me moaning over the uselessness of trying to survive in the path of glamor and beauty, for I have lost both of these elements during the course of the years, yet my talent has no end in sight and yet I am not judged by this but by the fullness of my breast. So long, guys, I will see all of you tomorrow if the lord is on my side . . . if not, send me no flowers . . . for I will venture to exploit all of me in that great casting office in the sky . . . bye . . .

DOMINICK: Who was she!

JOE THE COP: I don't know her name, but by the silver tongue that she left behind, she must be the stone ranger . . .

JOE: That's nice, Joe. See you next time.

JOE THE COP: Good night, Joe, Gerry, Mr. er, er???

FRED: Fred, Fred Pulley. Call me Fred.

JOE THE COP: Good night, Fred . . . and Dominick, don't do nothing I wouldn't do. *(Joe the Cop exits.)*

JOE: So long, Joe. Nice guy. One of the really decent cops on the force.

GERRY: He's all right for a cop.

JOE: All cops are really all right. They have a tremendous job on their hands when they become New York City cops.

GERRY: Don't I know it. Don't forget my oldest one is a cop.

DOMINICK: Why did Officer Joe say that to me?

JOE: Say what?

DOMINICK: That I shouldn't do nothing he wouldn't do. I don't know what he wouldn't do, so how am I going to know if I am doing something that he wouldn't do?

JOE: You know, as crazy as that may sound, it makes sense. But even

. . . look, that's just an old American saying, Dom.

DOMINICK: It doesn't make any sense to me.

GERRY: You mean you never heard it said before, Dom?

JOE: If he had, would he be acting like he hadn't?

GERRY: Just surprised, that's all. (*Telephone rings.*)

DOMINICK: I got it.

JOE: I'll get it. City Morgue, you stab 'em, we slab 'em. Oh, hi Ruth. Sorry, can't make no deliveries today. The boy didn't show. Yeah, yeah, I know this is the second day in a row, but what can I tell you? Listen, order from someone else. No, no hard feelings whatsoever, okay, bye . . . the bitch.

GERRY: Who was that?

JOE: Ruth Singerton from up the street. She's really got a whole lot of nerve, hasn't she?

GERRY: She has a whole lot of something else too.

JOE: She sure does. That woman has a future behind her.

FRED: Well, here you are, Joe.

JOE: Leaving already?

FRED: Yeah, got to get back to work. You know some people work while others pretend to work, right, Gerry?

GERRY: I wouldn't know, I'm only here eight hours a day.

FRED: Aaah, you bum. Take it easy you bums.

JOE: You too, you bum.

DOMINICK: Good night, Mr. Pulley.

FRED: Hey, call me Fred.

DOMINICK: Right, Fred . . . bye.

GERRY: Get out of here already you bum.

FRED: Let me get a pack of Camels.

JOE: Here you are, on the house.

GERRY: Yeah, we like giving away coffin nails.

FRED: Ahhh, you bum. So long, see you tomorrow.

JOE: Okay, Fred. (*Fred exits.*)

GERRY: How old you think Fred is?

JOE: He's past sixty-five I think.

GERRY: He's a baby compared to you, heh Joe?

JOE: Blow that our your ass.

DOMINICK: What about the delivery boy, Joe?

JOE: What delivery boy? He's fired.

DOMINICK: My cousin, Aristotle, is looking for work. He's young and strong.

JOE: Bring him around tomorrow and I'll have a look at him.

GERRY: What are you now, a casting director . . .

DOMINICK: What's a casting director, Joe?

GERRY: What do you wanna eat, Dominick? . . . I'll make it for you.

DOMINICK: Eggs and tomatoes.

GERRY: You want some coffee?

DOMINICK: Yes. No, today, tea with lemon.

JOE: A casting director, it's a job in the entertainment business.

GERRY: The entertainment business?

JOE: It's a business!

GERRY: Gee, Joe, I'm only kidding.

JOE: Well I don't take it as a joke.

GERRY: Okay, okay, sorry that I try to be human.

DOMINICK: What's wrong? Why are you two fighting?

GERRY: He was an entertainer most of his life.

DOMINICK: A what?

JOE: I was in show business. That's why I bought this place. Never played Broadway, so when I got too old to make the rounds regularly I decided, well I may never play Broadway, so let me work on Broadway. So me and three other friends of mine bought this here place and settled down to relax our few years on this earth with the toil of good, honest, hard work. I'm the only one left of the three. Gerry just bought a share of the place, makes him a partner now. But he worked in this place for a long time before he could make enough money to buy a share of the place. Dominick, there's plenty of opportunity in America to make a decent living if you put your mind to it. I mean don't think that it's been easy for anybody. When you get right down to it, Dominick, there are very few people in this country who were born with a silver spoon in their mouth. Most of us got to where we are today by getting up every morning and reporting to work and by saving a pretty penny here, a pretty penny there, until you find that you have enough to make a lot of pretty pennies to work for you. You should work hard for the dollar and then sit back and relax and let the dollar work hard for you. That's the way to live in America. I mean I really don't understand all this bitching that goes on in the newspapers every day. The Negro and the Puerto Ricans and now the Cubans and Vietnamese, we let them in this country to do something for themselves and they expect the country to feed them and clothe them and lead them by the hand until they can find some type of education, looking for a handout. They don't want to work.

DOMINICK: Do not ask what your country can do for you, ask what you can do for your country.

JOE: Exactly. Hey that's pretty clever.

DOMINICK: John F. Kennedy said it in a speech.

JOE: He did, huh? . . . smart your man. I still think he was too young to run a country like this one. Not enough experience in high political office. There's a lot of sharpies up there. Dominick, you go to night school right, and you read the papers, what's your opinion?

GERRY: Not that it matters any.

JOE: Come on, be serious. Soon this man is going to be a citizen of this country and he should know that he can express his political, religious and social views without fear of persecution.

DOMINICK: Well you know, Joe, I lived over there and I lived in many places that you call over there.

GERRY: (Singing.) Over there, over there. Tell 'em that the yanks are coming. The yanks are coming over there.

JOE: That's un-American, Gerry. If you make fun of those songs that inspired men to fight for freedom of the world, you might as well spit on the flag and curse the President.

GERRY: Damn, Joe, I was only kidding, you kid around too.

JOE: Yeah, but when I do, it's different.

GERRY: What's so different about it?

JOE: Because when I do it, I do it as a showman. You're not a showman, a stand-up comic; I was.

GERRY: Like you was not like you are.

JOE: Let me tell you how it was when we got to Paris during the big one.

GERRY: We know how it was, Joe.

DOMINICK: I read about it in school.

JOE: Yeah, but reading about it is not the same as hearing about it. Them French girls, my God were they the horniest broads that I ever met in my life. They rip your pants off if they caught you in the streets or in a hotel room. Man, they were sure the horniest broads in my life. One thing I can say for the French is that their women sure taught me a mess of things about women.

GERRY: I have something to say about the French too. The French is a wonderful race polly boo.

JOE: Ahahaha . . . the French is a wonderful race polly boo.

JOE and GERRY: (Singing together to Dominick.)
The French is a wonderful race polly boo . . .

The French is a wonderful race polly boo . . .
The French is a wonderful race
they fight with their feet
and fuck with their face.
Hinky, dinky, pollyyy booo.

JOE: I haven't sang that since Paris, my, my, how time has slipped right on by.

GERRY: What was the other Polly Boo song that we used to sing.

JOE: Oh, right, let me see, the first marine bought the beans.

GERRY: Polly boo . . . come Dominick, just say polly boo, okay?

JOE: The second marine cooked the beans.

GERRY and DOMINICK: Polly boo.

JOE: The third marine ate the beans and shitted all over the submarine.

JOE and GERRY and DOMINICK: Hinky dinky, polly boooo.

JOE: Let's stop it, too much.

GERRY: Joe, you all right?

JOE: Yeah, I'm all right.

GERRY: Joe, why don't you go to Paris?

JOE: It would be nice, wouldn't it.

GERRY: It'll be great. You and me, the kids are all grown up and they, well, you know they . . .

JOE: They don't need us anymore.

GERRY: Sometimes I think I'm in their way. They were talking about putting me in an old age home.

JOE: So that's why you moved away?

GERRY: Yeah, that's why. (*Telephone rings.*)

JOE: This is the house of the Lord, Moses is speaking. Oh hello, Ruth . . . it's that Singerton broad again. Yeah, Dominick, you feel like making a delivery?

DOMINICK: Sure, why not. Do I get a tip?

JOE: Yeah, don't bet on the horses . . . ahahahaha.

GERRY: What you want me to cook up, Joe?

JOE: The regular thing.

GERRY: Four coffees, two light no sugar, one black, one regular, two danishes, one neopolitan, one eclair, one french cruller and we'll throw in one corn muffin.

DOMINICK: What is the address?

JOE: Here ya are and don't stay there all night googling at her ass.

GERRY and JOE: (*Singing.*)
Barney Google with the goo goo googly eyes

Barney Google with a wife three times his size
She sued Barney for divorce
Then she ran off with his horse
Barney Google with the goo goo googly eyes.

GERRY: Take the umbrella, it's drizzling out there.

JOE: Hey, Dominick, don't get wet.

DOMINICK: Thanks.

JOE: So that's why you moved out, heh?

GERRY: Yeah, I didn't understand their insistence on them putting me in a prison away from all the love and care that I can give them. I know that they mean well, but that kind of well meaning I can do without. I'm not a cripple, Joe, I drive my own car. I supported them until they were old enough to make it out here in the jungle by themselves. Like I did, I paved the road with education, the education that I was not lucky enough to get. Sure they would come and see me once or twice a week, maybe every day for a while and how long do you think that would last? Have you ever seen a home for the aged? It's a death life, all these living beings wrinkled and feeble and mumbling to themselves, holding on to the last postcard from other couples' children, imagining that they are their own grand kids. Decaying photographs of themselves inside handmade frames, that helped for awhile, too many homes, private ones, state owned, some of them real fancy names with chandeliers and candles burning. Others were brutal in themselves, home for the aged and the feeble. What can you do, when you reach the point of fear, of helplessness? A little money keeps you alive inside yourself. And then they want to take it all away from you, for your own good, for their own sense of privacy is more like it, Joe, for their sense of insanity that pushes them into being social workers rather than the children that you brought up and struggled and fought for all your life. If I didn't put them in an institution when they were young, why do they want to do it to me because I'm old? They rate me obsolete, that's what it is, Joe, they rate us obsolete. We hold no more useful function in their lives. I wonder what would happen if someday they come to that realization about all of us . . . When they figure that keeping us in a home is very expensive, would they just feed us into the gas chambers like Hitler did those poor miserable Jews? Would they all leave and give us a piece of earth to toil until we are dead? Maybe they will create dead end jobs that serve the same function that we do, none. You know when Lyndon Johnson retired to his ranch in Texas, I thought that he would be like the rest of the retired presidents of this nation and die along with the headlines in a garbage can. Then I saw a picture of him in the *Daily News* riding a horse and wearing his hair as long as the very people who protested his stay in office and his policies. What do you think he was telling the world, a retired President of the greatest nation on earth wearing his hair like that? It was almost like a sign of arrogance, of protest, against the talk that he was old and ready to die any moment. Joe, I haven't seen my children or my grandchildren since Martha and I moved out of the house to be on our own. They said that I was insane and . . . oh shit, I miss the hell out of them, Joe. I love my children like I never loved anything else in this world, and watching and helping to take care of their children was like reliving the past with them all over again. Me and Martha would take them out and spoil the hell out of them, but it was a good kind of spoiling, the good kind, and they used that to try to commit me. I miss them, Joe, and I know that I'll never see them again, because I, Joe, I have made that decision myself. Joe, sometimes I feel like . . . *(He begins to sing.)* Sometimes I feel like a motherless child . . . *(Nightlife, a young man of twenty, enters.)*

NIGHTLIFE: Hi, my it's getting cold out there. Hardly no people on the streets . . . *(He pops a quarter in the jukebox.)* It's a good day for a mugging. *(Stevie Wonder's "Living for the City" comes up on the jukebox.)*

JOE: If that's your work I guess it is. What'll it be?

MAN: Give me a chocolate malted milk.

GERRY: *(Exiting to the kitchen.)* One chocolate malted, coming up. *(Nightlife begins to boogie to the music.)*

NIGHTLIFE: Is that chocolate cream pie?

JOE: Yep, fresh chocolate cream pie.

NIGHTLIFE: *(Still boogying.)* How much a slice?

JOE: Forty-five cents.

NIGHTLIFE: Let me get those two pieces.

JOE: Both of them?

NIGHTLIFE: Yeah, both of them, do you mind?

JOE: You're paying for them. You're eating them, so why should I mind? You want them now?

NIGHTLIFE: Yeah, now, thanks. *(Nightlife begins to stuff the pie into his mouth.)*

JOE: You like pie, huh?

NIGHTLIFE: Yeah, I like pies.

JOE: Good, huh?

NIGHTLIFE: Good. *(After a beat.)* You happen to know what time it is?

JOE: The clock is on the wall behind you.

NIGHTLIFE: Man, I didn't know it was so early. I works late, they call me Nightlife.

JOE: It's a name.

NIGHTLIFE: Can I read that paper until the malt is ready?

JOE: Sure, why not, here. *(As Joe folds up the paper, Nightlife boogies to the kitchen door and peers into the back.)*

JOE: You expecting someone else?

NIGHTLIFE: Why?

JOE: Just that you keep looking around to see if anyone is there.

NIGHTLIFE: Maybe I'm trying to make sure that *no one* is there.

JOE: Maybe.

NIGHTLIFE: How's this business, you make a good dollar?

JOE: We do all right.

GERRY: *(Entering from the kitchen.)* Here's your chocolate malt, sonny.,

NIGHTLIFE: Nightlife is my name.

GERRY: *(Putting the malt on the counter in front of Nightlife.)* I call people by their names if they are my friends or are about to be my friends.

NIGHTLIFE: Yeah, that's cool. *(He drinks the malt down in one long gulp.)* You make a nice malted milk.

GERRY: Thanks, I try.

NIGHTLIFE: Don't we all.

JOE: *(Slapping a check in front of Nightlife.)* That'll be a dollar sixty-five.

NIGHTLIFE: I got eyes, I can see, thank you. *(The three of them stare at each other for a moment, then Nightlife takes out a cigarette, looks at Joe and Gerry with an exaggerated villainous smile. He gets up with one hand in his pocket and performs a whole silent movie bad guy routine of curling his mustache and giving the Richard Widmark crazy killer laugh. He then remains in total silence for a long moment, then yells out "BOO" slapping the counter with two dollars. Joe pulls out a large revolver and Gerry has a meat cleaver at the ready. Nightlife begins to laugh at them hysterically. Joe takes the money, gives Nightlife his change, refuses the tip. Nightlife leaves, laughing his way out the door. Two men, Reynolds and Lockhart, enter the place along with Joe the Cop.)*

JOE: Hey, Joe, what brings you around?

GERRY: Hey Joe, what happened to the desk job?

JOE THE COP: This is business, Gerry.

JOE: Police business in our place?

GERRY: I told you they'd catch up with you sooner or later, Dillinger.

JOE THE COP: These two men are from the Government.

REYNOLDS: Reynolds, Federal Bureau of Investigation.

LOCKHART: Lockhart, Bureau of Immigration.

REYNOLDS: Joseph Scott, you own the place?

JOE: Yeah, that's right. We own the place. It's a legal business. There's nothing going on in this place that ain't legal. I'm an honest man.

GERRY: Gerald Fisher is my name. I'm part owner here. What's the trouble?

REYNOLDS: There's no trouble with either of you.

LOCKHART: We're looking for a Mister Dominick Athemus Skorpios.

JOE: Dominick? What's he done?

LOCKHART: He's in the country illegally.

GERRY: That's not true! He's an American citizen . . . by marriage.

REYNOLDS: We know of his marriage to one Carmen de Jesus— also known as Iris Morales-Milagros Ramirez. She has a list of aliases that can go on for a couple of days and we don't have much time.

JOE: Well, I don't know how many names she has, nor do I care if she is an American citizen by birth.

JOE THE COP: Easy, Joe. Will ya hear them out first before you blow a fuse.

GERRY: She is a Puerto Rican—she's a citizen by birth.

JOE: Yeah, what ya mean? That Puerto Ricans aren't citizens of this country? They are one of the finest people to ever set foot in this God-given soil.

REYNOLDS: Puerto Ricans are citzens, sir.

LOCKHART: But not Mexicans, Mr. Scott.

JOE: Mexican?

GERRY: Mexican? What ya mean? She's a Mex? . . . She showed us her birth certificate.

LOCKHART: Phony. Most of her papers are phonies.

REYNOLDS: Where's Mister Skorpios now?

JOE: He's out making a delivery . . . He'll be back soon.

REYNOLDS: Good, we'll wait.

JOE THE COP: See, Joe, it's like this. This dame goes around posing as Puerto Rican so that she can hook fishes like Dominick into paying her to marry her so they can stay in the country through marriage.

LOCKHART: We have her in custody now. Mister Skorpios may have to face other charges of conspiracy. So his chances to have stayed here are less even with the help you may offer in his behalf.

REYNOLDS: Lockhart, call in.

LOCKHART: Will do.

GERRY: Oh, poor Dominick. (Enter Dominick.)

DOMINICK: Hell, Joe, here's the money. She gave me no tip. She's cheap, ain't she?

JOE: Isn't she. It's "isn't she." These two men are here to see you, Dom. They're from the government. They wanna talk to you about . . . hell, Gerry, you tell him.

GERRY: They say you are here illegally and they . . . well, they . . .

DOMINICK: Illegally? No that's not true anymore. I'm married to an American. I got married to an American. I'm not . . .

JOE: That's just it. She's not an American. She's not a Puerto Rican. She's a wetback Mexican scab who slipped into the country and took all of us in . . . goddamn it, Dominick . . . goddamn her soul.

DOMINICK: She not an American?

LOCKHART: I'm afraid not, Mr. Skorpios.

REYNOLDS: Let's go. We can talk about this downtown.

DOMINICK: Wait please! I just want to live here to make a life here, like your fathers did. Like Joe says, I would, if I work hard enough at it. I want to make my life here, to make a decent living here in America. Can't I stay? Can't I stay please! Let me stay here in this place. I work hard, ask Joe . . . ask Gerry . . . I'm never late, never did I miss a day of work, always I work late and hard and very much. Never am I lazy.

REYNOLDS: Let's go.

DOMINICK: I do not ask for welfare or any kind of help from government . . . just to let me make a life here. I just want to be an American.

JOE THE COP: I'm sorry, Dominick.

JOE: It's not your fault, Joe. It's all our faults.

REYNOLDS: Come along, Mr. Skorpios. Good night, gentlemen.

LOCKHART: Good night, sorry, we're just doing out job . . . you understand.

JOE: We understand . . . yeah, we understand. (*Exit Reynolds, Lockhart and Dominick.*)

GERRY: Poor Dominick. He didn't even get laid . . . (*Lights out.*)

ACT II

Same scene. Three hours later, it is the height of the hour Joe and Gerry are busy serving the customers. Zulma enters during the scene and sips on a cup of chocolate. The scene as originally produced was improvised around the following set of characters: Man One, Man Two, Hooker One, Hooker Two, Cowboy. At the end of the scene, the Hookers exit with Cowboy. Gerry turns to Joe.

GERRY: (*Pointing to Junkie Girl.*) Hey, Joe.

JOE: She's pulling a Mary Hartman–Mary Hartman.

GIRL: Hey, wow, Mary Hartman. I look like Mary Hartman?

JOE: No.

GERRY: What he's saying is you're pulling a Mary Hartman.

GIRL: How's that?

JOE: Drowning in a bowl of soup.

GIRL: This soup is cold. I don't want it.

JOE: You pay for it just the same.

GIRL: Hey, yeah, wow, like I got bread. (*Throws her money on the counter and stumbles out into the night. The Shopping Bag Lady sits on a stool mumbling to herself, hell, damn, fuck you, shit, bastard. Profanity is the only thing she says.*)

LADY: Mumble mumble Damn you mumble mumble. (*Waving her hands all the time, she takes the things from time to time and puts them inside her shopping bag. She exits during the song "Greasy Spoon Blues."*)

GERRY: Goddamn it, wouldn't you know it, Joe, that today would turn out to be busier than usual? Just our luck to have Dominick picked up at the height of the hour.

JOE: Poor Dominick. He should have called in sick.

GERRY: Aw, they would have turned up tomorrow or the next day. When the Feds are after you, forget it. You can run, but you can't hide. That's the old saying about them. Dillinger found that out. So did Babyface Nelson and Ma Barker and a host of others that fled the F.B.I. You just can't win. It's like playing a game of stud poker and knowing that the deck is stacked against you, but you sit down to play anyway, that's the philosophy of the criminal mind. They go out and play against a stacked deck. It's a means of ending the beginning of yourself.

JOE: Well, you know what they say about destiny.

GERRY: No, I don't. What is it they say about destiny?

JOE: How should I know? I thought you knew. (*Telephone rings.*)

JOE: There's a midnight moon at the greasy spoon tonight. Oh . . . hi, Ruth. What can I do for you? . . . Who? Oh, Dominick . . . naw, he ain't here anymore. They took him away today . . . Who? The F.B.I., that's who . . . they found out he was a wanted killer. . . . Yeah, they got wind of him from the C.I.A. They spotted him and turned him over to the C.I.D., who turned him over to the B.C.I., who called Scotland Yard, who called Interpol, who called the F.B.I. and they came and took him away. . . . That's right. A born killer, they said. . . . Yep, about twenty people with a rusty ax handle . . . no motive. He did it for pleasure . . . what? . . . no . . . throughout the nation, yep, been underground for years. Sure we knew about it. Gerry thought he could rehabilitate him. . . . No, I'm not lying to you. . . . You wanna ask Gerry? . . . Sure, it's the truth. . . . Yep, twenty people . . . mostly late night working women. . . . Yep, late night working women. . . . Naw, no men . . . just women . . . in their late forties. Seems he had a kind of psycho thing about him, always when he delivered coffee to them. You sure are lucky . . . he's not going to be able to keep that date. Yeah, it's really a shame. . . . Take it easy. . . . No, there's no chance of him escaping. But if he does, you will be the first to know. . . . Yeah, he talked about you a lot. Yeah, I think you should go to bed. Yeah, that's not a bad idea. . . . Sure will. Good night. Pleasant dreams. . . . Bye. . . . Chiao . . . hang up already, will you! . . . Damn, that woman sure can be a pain in the lower back. . . . Boy, one of these days. One of these days . . .

GERRY: I'll bet she'll dream of Dominick tonight.

JOE: I bet she will.

GERRY: Twenty people with a rusty ax handle . . . that's a good one.

JOE: Mostly late night working women . . .

ZULMA: (*Stands up slowly.*) You guys had a killer working here . . . trying to rehabilitate a born killer. That guy Dominick was a killer? He sure didn't look like a killer. He didn't look like a killer. He didn't act like a killer. And he didn't talk like a killer. (*Pause.*) But then again, what does a killer look like or what does a killer say to someone when they first meet. Hi, I'm a killer.

JOE: Zelma, he was no killer. Believe me, I was joking with that women.

ZULMA: The name is Zulma, not Zelma.

JOE: Zulma out here and Zelma at home.

ZULMA: It's Zulma out here and Zulma at home and Zulma on stage and Zulma in here.

JOE: Zulma. Zelma. Zulma. Zelma. Zelma. Zulma. What's in a name?

ZULMA: Plenty.

GERRY: So how's business?

ZULMA: Do you know what? This morning I went to five auditions. Count them. Five. Since this morning I've been pounding the concrete, making the rounds and all I got is the same "don't call us, we'll call you" routine.

JOE: Oh, how I know them words so well.

ZULMA: Oh, I bet you know the routine.

GERRY: But with a name like Zulma Samson, well you know, what you can expect?

ZULMA: It has nothing to do with the name, Gerry. It's the age . . . the age. It's the age. (*She begins to weep.*)

JOE: Hey! Hey, look, don't do that. Come on now, pull yourself together. come on, Zulma, not in here. What if someone comes in? Look, stop crying, will ya? . . . please stop crying.

ZULMA: It's the age. It's the age. I'm a has-been . . . a has-been that never was. I was once so beautiful, to look at me you wouldn't think so, but I was. I was once so beautiful . . . what's happened to me . . . ?

JOE: You're still beautiful. You still got a lot of spunk left in you. Stop crying.

ZULMA: Oh, stop it. I know the truth. I know the truth, that's why I'm crying, 'cause I know the truth . . . I realize the truth. I can't hide from the mirror anymore. My time is over. My time is over and I never even got to look at the clock of success. . . . I'm passed the hour of life. . . . I can face the truth now . . . I can face all the wrinkles without all the make-up. I can face it now . . . I know that I'm all washed up . . . but what am I going to do? . . . What am I going to do . . .? I know nothing else but show business . . . it's all I know since I was a child. And I am not going to end up in no old actors home to tell stories of glorious events that never took place . . . lay by the window all the time watching the sunrise . . . hoping that each ray of light will bring in a letter from Dino de Laurentis or a script hand-delivered from Joseph Papp saying that he needs me to play the lead in a new production at Lincoln Center . . . no . . . no . . . no actors home for me. . . . I was born on stage . . . well, not exactly on stage, it was a traveling show in a tent. I was on stage when the final labor pain struck my mother . . . no, I know nothing else, and I never wanted to know anything else but what I know . . . and it's been grand and I want to remember it as being grand and I always, since the moment I was able to fend for myself . . . I've took care of myself and now I've reached the ebb of my tide . . .

GERRY: "The ebb of my tide" . . . Zulma, you're really a ham.

ZULMA: Of the finest caliber.

JOE: So, now that you say you know what you think is the truth of your final years on the good earth, what do you plan on doing with them?

GERRY: How do you plan to support yourself?

ZULMA: I'll get me a steady job.

JOE: You have any place in mind?

ZULMA: Sure.

JOE: Where?

ZULMA: Here.

GERRY: Where?

ZULMA: Here.

JOE: Here!

ZULMA: Here.

GERRY: Did she say here?

ZULMA: What are you guys . . . a comedy team?

GERRY: She did say here.

ZULMA: I thought I was clear about that.

JOE: I know you sounded clear and I know that you think you sounded clear, but I wanted to make sure that you sounded clear about being clear about working here . . . I mean, I don't want to sound as if I and Gerry were a large firm, but we feel somehow that since we are going to have to pay wages to whoever spends hours here . . .

ZULMA: What's the problem? I mean, look, you like me and I like you. . . . You do like me???

JOE: Sure.

GERRY: No one said that they didn't like you, at least I didn't.

JOE: I didn't say it either.

ZULMA: Okay, then what's the problem? You like me, I like you, we can have a beautiful working relationship. And it's close to Broadway, you know what I mean.

JOE: I know what you mean, more than you think.

GERRY: Well, it's okay with me if it's okay with Joe.

JOE: Well, if it's okay with you, then it's okay with me.

GERRY: When can you start?

ZULMA: Nothing like the present for doing what you have to do, right fellas?!

GERRY: Right!

JOE: Go in the back and put on something that'll keep the grease off your clothes.

ZULMA: Oh, by the way. I look ridiculous in a mini-skirt, so I hope you don't require that your female workers wear one.

JOE: I wouldn't dream of asking you to wear one.

ZULMA: Look at that. Not even in your dreams can you see me in a mini-skirt. Boy, I must look worse than I thought.

JOE: I didn't mean it that way.

ZULMA: No? In what way then?

JOE: Just go get somethin' on, will ya? (*Zulma exits to the kitchen.*)

GERRY: She's okay, you know . . . a regular guy.

JOE: Yeah, she's all right. I'm glad that she's getting a little more sense into her head nowadays. You know, I think we're going to have a nice night tomorrow.

GERRY: Yeah, I think so too . . . though, I still feel sorry for poor old Dominick.

JOE: Yeah, I think I'm going to miss him too.

GERRY: He would have made a great American citizen.

JOE: Just like you, huh?

GERRY: Yeah, just like me . . . What??!! You think that I'm not a great American citizen?

JOE: No, I don't think you're a great American citizen.

GERRY: You don't?

JOE: No, I don't think you're a great American citizen.

GERRY: You're kidding.

JOE: No, I'm serious.

GERRY: What you think, I'm some kinda pinko fag commie or something?

JOE: No, I don't think you're some kinda pinko fag commie or something.

GERRY: Then what do you mean by saying that I'm not a great American citizen?

JOE: Gerry, I think you're a *good* American citizen. I think you're a patriotic American citizen. I think you're a loyal American citizen. But I don't think you're a great American citizen. Greatness is reserved for those who do not make their living being a short order cook.

GERRY: Greatness is not reserved, Joe. Greatness is there for all who wish to claim it. I for one never had the passion to grab it and the responsibilities that go along with it. I am a simple man . . . a humble man . . . a man of wisdom, of worldly knowledge . . . of compassion . . . (*Enter a Young Musician and his Girlfriend.*)

GIRL: You tell 'em.

BOY: You tell 'em.

GIRL: Why did you tell me you was going to tell 'em if you ain't going to tell 'em?

BOY: I said I *might* tell 'em today.

GIRL: Well, tomorrow is the gig and we promised to tell 'em if we got the job. Right! So tell 'em!

BOY: Yeah, if . . .

GIRL: No ifs, ands or buts about it . . . Joe . . .

JOE: Yeah.

GIRL: Can we see you for a sec?

JOE: Hey, Gerry, you wanna handle the old lady. I want to talk with the kids.

GERRY: No skin off my nose . . .

JOE: Hey, kids, how's the business treating you?

BOY: Well, I think we got a gig.

JOE: No kidding.

GIRL: Well, it's not much of a gig . . .

BOY: It's in the West Village.

GIRL: But it's a start.

JOE: A start, no matter how big or small, it's a start. What'a ya wanna eat?

BOY: Boy, I'm too excited to talk or sleep *or eat.*

GIRL: I never thought we could make it here in the concrete cold,

72

metal monster, but it looks like it might happen.

JOE: Yeah, no time at all you might be another Sonny and weird.

GIRL: You mean Cher.

JOE: That's just what I said, weird.

GIRL: I hope it happens soon. Our phone has been disconnected, the rent is due and we owe you almost twenty dollars.

BOY: We wanted you to know that we are singing at this place 'cause they're putting up posters announcing our appearance and we didn't want you to think that we are making money and eating for free.

JOE: Yeah, but you're playing for free.

GIRL: We wrote . . . well, he wrote a song for you and the place.

BOY: Yeah, we wanna dedicate this song to you and Gerry.

GERRY: For us?

BOY: Hunh, yeah.

GIRL: You've been so wonderful, we needed encouragement and you gave it.

GERRY: Hey, what time is the performance? Maybe we can make it.

JOE: You know those things happen at night.

BOY: Yeah, too bad 'cause we would really dig it if you showed up at the joint.

GIRL: Well, we better be going if we are going to be wide awake for the gig.

JOE: Not until we hear our song.

GERRY: Right, since you can't pay us the money you owe, ya gotta play Tommy Tucker and sing for your supper.

GIRL: You want me to sing?

BOY: You got the voice.

GIRL: Well, I don't know . . .

JOE: What's there to know? Look at it this way, it's a rehearsal before the performance tomorrow.

GIRL: All right.

BOY: Are you ready, Cher?

GIRL: Yes, Sonny.

LADY: Fuck you, mumble, mumble . . .

GERRY: (To Shopping Bag Lady.) Please sweety.

JOE: Forget about her, she isn't listening or talking to anyone here but herself. Go ahead, kids. (The song, Greasy Spoon Blues. Words and music by Charles Coker. During the song the Shopping Bag Lady exits, mumbling profanities to whomever is listening.)

GIRL: Bye, Joe.

JOE: Bye, kids. Break a leg tomorrow. (*Jake enters.*)

GERRY: Yeah, break a leg.

JAKE: Hey, nigger, what's happening?

JOE: Jake, why do you always call me a nigger?

JAKE: Because you are.

GERRY: Hi, Jake, how's the parlor business coming along?

JAKE: Great, can't do better if I try. I just got me two new girls.

GERRY: Black?

JAKE: Two tall Swedish blondes that are looking sweeter than a piece of watermelon on a hot sticky day in the city.

JOE: Two blondes, huh?

JAKE: Two blondes.

GERRY: Two tall blondes?

JAKE: Yep, two tall blondes.

JOE: Blondes, huh?

JAKE: Two tall big-tit blondes that are for real. I mean it ain't dye either. That yellow goldness is for real . . . it's natural . . . I know cause they got that yellow hair everywhere else too.

GERRY: Natural blondes, huh?!

JAKE: Natural blondes.

JOE: They got yellow hair everywhere else?

JAKE: All over!

GERRY: All over?

JAKE: Boy, I wish I had a tape recorder with me.

GERRY: A tape recorder, what in heavens name for?

JAKE: To get this all down for posterity. You guys sound like a couple of typical out of town businessmen in a cathouse.

JOE: Well, we are a couple of businessmen, not from out of town, but businessmen nevertheless. You know, Jake, we weren't exactly raised with the same disadvantages that you had to endure.

JAKE: What disadvantages are you talking about?

GERRY: Yeah, cause I would also like to know.

JOE: You know what I mean . . . this whole production number that you had to undergo since the curtain rose on your act . . . not having the same education that I and Gerry were fortunate enough to have, even though I never really finished high school, only because of the fact that I was the oldest of the family, and when my father died in the war I had to go out into the wide rushings of making a daily living for the rest of the kids, not that I'm complaining, you know, I mean, I loved doing what I did . . . show biz is my cup of tea, every penny that I earned from hoofing

74

it up, wherever the show boat stopped, went back home . . . and
. . .

GERRY: I thought you were an orphan, Joe.

JOE: There you go again, Gerry, everytime that I have this nigger by the balls, hanging onto every word, there you go again breaking up the story.

JAKE: Joe . . . fifteen years . . .

JOE: Yeah, it's been fifteen years. Well, what about it?

JAKE: Do you think that I was really going for that cock'n'bull yarn you were spinning?

JOE: I'm sure that if this klondike over here hadn't of interrupted, you would've been standing there with your tongue hanging out, hanging, yeah . . . yeah . . . and what happened next, Joe . . .?

JAKE: Joe, come on off it.

JOE: Jake, I made my living spinning yarns to suckers like you.

JAKE: What kind of a car you drive, Joe?

JOE: You know what kind of a car I drive.

GERRY: Yeah, you gave it to him last Christmas.

JAKE: That's not what I'm saying, Gerry.

JOE: Well, if you are going to flaunt that present in my face and in front of strangers . . .

GERRY: Strangers? Who's a stranger here?

JOE: Gerry, why don't you go in the back and do something?

JAKE: Yeah, Gerry, why don't you go take some meat in the back.

GERRY: Why don't both of you get yourselves a nice job in a balloon factory blowing . . .?

JAKE: As you were saying, Joe.

JOE: If you are going to flaunt that present in my face in front of strangers, then I suggest that you get me a Cadillac instead of that cheap second-hand station wagon that I drive from Honest Harry.

JAKE: Joe, I drive a Cadillac on Tuesdays and Thursdays. On Fridays and Sundays, while I relax in my country home, I fool around with my Porsche and sometimes I even get a big kick by returning to this God-forsaken city in my Honda. So you see, Joe, all that bull about my disadvantaged childhood is just a lot of hot air blowing out your mouth. Actually, it's a substitute for the bottom part of your body. (*Gerry laughs.*)

JOE: It ain't that funny, Gerry.

GERRY: You're big, Joe. The truth isn't always funny, but with you it's a riot.

JOE: Careful how you use that word around Jake, 'cause you know what they say . . . you can take the nigger out of the country but . . .

JAKE: You can't take the country out of the nigger and you know where that comes from, Joe.

JOE: Sure, from where all sayings come from . . . wise thinking of a man of wisdom.

JAKE: No. Not from any great man of wisdom, but from a truth that all niggers know about this country.

GERRY: What truth, Jake?

JOE: Don't fall for it, Gerry, he's pulling the same routine I pulled on him.

JAKE: It's not a routine, Joe, it's the real thing. Here we are reaching the heights of our existing on this planet . . . two hundred years old . . . we've just celebrated the birth of a freedom revolution that ceased being a revolution for freedom twenty-four hours after its conception. . . . As the years rolled by and the mentality of this country remained stagnant, the niggers in this country became angrier and angrier as they paid in blood in countless wars that cried out the words of liberty, justice and equality. We found ourselves being booed over and over again, no matter how many times we fought and died and bled in other lands for the sake of free enterprise and yet couldn't share in the profits . . . a free nation, a free people dedicated to the thought that all men are created equal up to the color of their skin, up to the pattern of your speech. Freedom became a whore, just like my ladies are. They're whores, but they're whores that admit they're whores and when the time comes that they know it doesn't benefit them to be whores any longer they change with the times and became respectable, quote unquote, "working women" with a family to raise. . . . Here . . . here we have a whore calling herself liberty-justice-and-equality. Oh, yeah, she's a whore, I can see by the look in your face, Joe, that you don't like what I am saying, but I am a spade who likes calling it as it plays, liberty is a whore, justice is a whore and equality is a faggot. How does that grab you? . . . She is a whore who spreads her legs to the highest bidder. Justice is blind to everyone but to those that spread over her eyelids the greed mercurochrome that heals all wounds. She sees, and liberty is once again that night your sleeping companion . . . the great average typical all-American dollar, that is the miracle worker, that is the real equalizer. If your pockets are hungry, so is your stomach and so is your soul. All that to say what we were saying: " You can take the niggers out of the country, but you can't take the country out of the nigger." All the niggers, white as well as black, the niggers who feel that they have a right to everything that this country has to offer them, the white niggers who built the railroads from the East, the yellow niggers who built the railroad from the West, the black niggers who built this land from all over, the rest of the niggers that died and crippled their lives so that all of us niggers can be a part of this great concept called America, land of the free. Death remembers the songs of false democracy. You understand what I am saying . . . it's like this . . . I remember after that prison rebellion in Attica . . . a politician said when Americans prefer to die than to live one more day in this country, it's time we start examining ourselves. I don't know if those were his exact words, but they had an effect on me. Joe, I did just that. I started to examine what my responsibilities were as a citizen of the greatest nation on the face of the earth. Am I or am I not . . . if I am, then it's time that I behave like one . . . how do you see yourself? . . .

JOE: I hope to see that I fulfill myself here everyday that the sun shines.

GERRY: So do I.

JOE: What brought this all about in you today, Jake?

JAKE: I don't know. Maybe it's reading that an eleven-year-old child O.D.'d in Harlem while an eleven-year-old in Scarsdale won the spelling bee for his district. Maybe it's age . . . maybe it's after knowing you fifteen years . . . you reacted pretty strange to the fact that I hired two white blonde girls to work in the parlor.

JOE: Wait a second . . . you didn't take me seriously, did you?

JAKE: Maybe I did without realizing it, maybe I did.

JOE: Well, you shouldn't, 'cause you know that I don't give a damn about who works for you or what their line of work is, as long as they respect me and what's mine.

GERRY: Yeah, you should know Joe better by now . . . fifteen years, damn if you don't.

JAKE: Yeah, and he even had dinner with me once in his home, his very own home, though he never came to my house to eat.

JOE: You know it could be because you never invited me, ever thought of that?

JAKE: Hell, that's right, I never did, did I?

JOE: No, you never did.

JAKE: And you know what, I never will.

JOE: The hell with you, you nigger.

GERRY: Things are back to normal.

JAKE: They always were.

JOE: That's great to hear.

GERRY: Two big-tit blondes, huh?

JAKE: Yep, two real big-tit blondes.

JOE: Yellow everywhere, huh?

JAKE: Yep, everywhere.

JOE: And they let you see it, huh?

JAKE: Well, if they didn't, they wouldn't be working for me, Joe.

JOE: Well, have they got any sense of shame?

JAKE: Why? 'Cause they are working in a massage parlor that's a front for a you-know-what or because they let a big black ugly nigger like me see their private parts, heh?

JOE: As for the first part of your question, if they want that kind of work, that's their business, not mine. To each his own, right Gerry?

JAKE: Don't ask Gerry, because he's been up there.

JOE: You have?

GERRY: Yeah, well . . . sure, but just out of curiosity.

JAKE: Out of what?

JOE: He said out of curiosity.

JAKE: I heard what he said, it's just that I couldn't believe that I heard what he said.

JOE: Repeat what you said for the gentleman, Gerry.

JAKE: He don't have to because you don't believe him and you know that I know you don't believe him.

GERRY: Hey, the *News* is here.

JOE: I'll get it.

JAKE: That's okay, Joe, relax, I'll bring them in for you.

JOE: *(Handing Jake a check.)* Here, Jake, give the driver this check for me.

JAKE: Sure . . . *(Jake exits.)*

JOE: How come you didn't tell me you were up at Jake's place?

GERRY: Well, Joe, you see, I was passing by one late afternoon, not having anything to do and well, you know, knowing Jake all these years and not ever being up to his place of business, well, I figure . . .

JOE: I know . . . I know . . . since he's such a good and steady customer, you wanted . . .

GERRY: Exactly . . .

JOE: One hand washes the other.

GERRY: Just what I was thinking on that very day.

JOE: I bet.

GERRY: Well, you know Joe, there's still a lot of something in this old man.

JOE: How was the merchandise? *(Jake enters.)*

JAKE: Here you are, Joe . . . let me take out five of these for my girls. They get bored after a while, you know, they need things, to read. I always believe that they should keep abreast of what's going on in the world . . . they need to have more to say to the customers.

GERRY: The merchandise is excellent, not like the rest of the trash out there.

JOE: Maybe I'll take a look-see.

JAKE: You should. That's always advisable at your age . . . see what you can handle before you get involved.

JOE: I don't remember asking for your advice, Mister Jake Andrews.

JAKE: Well, normally, Jake Andrews Esquire requires a small fee for advice, but since we're such bosom buddies, I thought I'd give it to you free of charge, but don't make it a habit.

JOE: That's the mistake of your career, Jake, you think . . . *(Zulma enters from the kitchen in her waitress outfit. She has removed her wig and cleaned the make-up off her face.)*

ZULMA: How's this, fellas?

JOE: Get back into the kitchen, there's talk going on in here that a woman shouldn't hear . . .

ZULMA: Oh, you got to be kidding. Hey, hi, Jake, how's the girls?

JAKE: Zulu baby . . . what're you doing in that get-up?

JOE: Zulu baby?

GERRY: Zulu baby?

ZULMA: There they go again.

JAKE: There who goes again?

ZULMA: The gold dust twins.

JOE: Zulu baby?

ZULMA: Yeah, Zulu! It's a nickname. Don't you guys have nicknames? . . . You know, like when you're a kid growing up and you get a name tagged on . . . Sinky . . . Tubby . . .

JAKE: These guys were born standing up.

JOE: But Zulu!

JAKE: And what's wrong with Zulu?

ZULMA: Yeah, what is wrong with Zulu? I like it, as a matter of fact.

GERRY: To each his own.

ZULMA: And what do you have?

JAKE: These guys haven't got nothing, but the lard in the frying pan to talk to.

JOE: At least if the lard is hot it tells you.

JAKE: It does, does it? . . . you talk to the lard? . . . little spoonfuls or big globs of it?

JOE: Oh, oh, oh very funny . . . very funny!!

GERRY: Five thousand comics out of work and he wants to be a comedian.

JAKE: I didn't think it was funny. I was asking a very serious question.

ZULMA: Yeah, he wasn't the one who said that he talks to the lard in the frying pan.

GERRY: You two should appear on stage at the Palace.

JOE: You two are really funny. I'll bet you'll be a regular hit with the drunks.

JAKE: I don't think we're funny. If I did, I would have tried the stage like you did.

JOE: Yeah, well I think that I am going . . .

JAKE: I saw you play the Lyric once when I was young.

JOE: You did? . . . you saw me on stage? . . .

JAKE: Sure did.

JOE: Really!

GERRY: Joe, he's trying to . . .

JOE: Be quiet, Gerry . . . can't you see the man is saying something important.

GERRY: Joe, he's only trying . . .

JAKE: No really, I did see him play on stage.

GERRY: Come on, you really expect me to believe that?

JAKE: He used to do a comic routine and then your partner would come on and do a soft shoe, right?

JOE: The Lyric . . . that was one of my favorite places.

JAKE: Am I right? You were billed as Jack and Jill.

JOE: That's right . . . gee, you remember . . . after all these years too.

JAKE: Oh, why wouldn't I remember. You were terrific.

JOE: Well, we was good.

JAKE: Good . . . you were great . . . everyone would just sit there after the movie and wait for you two to come on with the real show.

JOE: The real show?

JAKE: Yeah man, the real show.

GERRY: You really saw him play at the Lyric?

JAKE: Sure, just before the war, I think. You know it's been a long time.

JOE: You know, when I was a kid I was brought up in an orphanage.

GERRY: No, I didn't know that.

JOE: My parents were killed in an automobile accident at the age of three.

GERRY: Gee, I bet that was tough on you.

JOE: No, not really, being so young I really didn't feel the loss that great.

JAKE: I lost my folks too, at an early age . . . didn't go to no orphanage, though, my grandmother raised me . . . and with an iron hand and the cord.

JOE: The cord I remember only too well, the hurt it can inflict on a young child.

JAKE: Especially if it's in the hands of strangers.

JOE: Especially in the hands of strangers.

GERRY: You two got a lot in common. (*Telephone rings.*)

ZULMA: I'll get it . . . Joe's Diner . . . sorry, no deliveries tonight . . . can't be helped . . . sorry . . . tomorrow . . . bye . . . you were saying Joe?

JOE: I was in the place a few years, couldn't get adopted . . . every Sunday in summer they would have an invited performer come to entertain the kids. Once these two black men came in and they were really funny, they made me forget all the heartaches that flowed inside my soul . . . I was never a cute kid, so no one would even take me home for the weekends . . . they came on stage and told some really funny stories and they did a song and dance number . . . I looked around me and saw all those smiling faces and I began to sing out loud with the two men on stage. They called me with them and I joined them in the song . . . not the dancing, though. I never seen anyone dance like those two guys did. Boy, they could really move . . . later that week they came back and visited with me. I was surprised, to say the least, when the administrator let them come in for the month they played in town and teach me their routine . . . that Fourth of July I went on stage with them and let me tell you, I was the happiest kid in the place . . . soon they left and I never saw them again . . . but I kept on practicing how to dance and tried different jokes and stories at night on the other kids. Soon, I never wanted to be anything else but an entertainer . . . but life being what it is, I found myself drifting as a short order cook . . . not that there's anything wrong with being a short order cook, especially being part owner . . . I always dreamt that I would . . . well, so many dreams . . . never growing old . . . ahead of death by two yards . . . yet . . . here I am . . . I can't even remember the routine that I used to do, I . . . I, well . . . life sometimes leaves no room for a celebration . . . your greatest moments become objects of torment . . . but I guess I should thank the Lord for each dream, even if the dream never came true, at least I had the opportunity to have dreams . . . you reach a certain time in life . . . you find yourself wandering about in countless acres of flowers and one day it dawns on you . . . butterflies . . . thousands and thousands of butterflies . . . butterflies . . . and no more flowers are growing . . . (*Zulma begins to sing "Moonlight Bay." Joe joins in. They do a vaudeville soft-shoe routine. Jake and Gerry hum along.*)

JAKE: A bit rusty . . .

JOE: Go screw yourself . . .

GERRY: What'll it be, Jake?

ZULMA: I'll make it . . . you'll be my first customer.

JAKE: Great . . . two coffees regular and a bacon and egg sandwich to go.

ZULMA: Two coffees and a B&E to travel, coming right up.

GERRY: Got it?

ZULMA: (*Exiting to kitchen.*) Got it.

JAKE: Then get it, already.

JOE: Hold your horses.

JAKE: Hey, what happened to Dominick? . . . that funny Greek guy you had working here?

JOE: He got picked up by the Feds.

JAKE: When?

GERRY: Earlier this evening.

JAKE: No shh . . . really, what for?

JOE: Naw, I'm not going to tell you.

JAKE: Hey, come on . . . all right, don't tell me . . . come on, tell me, what for?

JOE: Seems Dominick was a top syndicate hit man. He was posing as a jerk to get closer to a certain psuedo-hip black, would-be king of the pimps.

GERRY: You know, Jake, you're the only man I know whose head is as pointed as his shoes.

JAKE: Okay. Enough! Hey, baby, don't burn the bacon. (*Goes to jukebox.*) Hey, you know my cousin Rufus . . . the one in the hospital?

JOE: Can't say I do.

JOE: No, seriously speaking.

JOE: Still can't say that I do.

GERRY: Never mentioned him to me either . . . Rufus . . . Rufus . . . with a name like that I would have remembered him if you had said anything about him.

JAKE: Sure I did . . . well, anyway, he was in the hospital for an operation . . . I forgot what was wrong with him . . . but, anyway . . . the doctors gave him an operation all right, they cut off both of his legs and there was nothing wrong with his legs. They made a mistake on the chart. Anyway, that's what they are saying . . . they cut both of his legs right above the knees, so he can't even walk.

GERRY: He's going to sue, right?

JOE: Of course, he's going to sue, he's got an open-and-shut case.

JAKE: Well, that's what we all thought until last week when we went to court and the jury didn't vote in his favor.

JOE: They didn't what?

GERRY: What do you mean, they didn't vote in his favor! They cut off both of the poor slob's legs and they found him . . .

JAKE: Yeah, I know the way you feel, but the court was right.

JOE: The court was right, what kind of crap is that?

GERRY: Yeah, what kind of crap is that? He should have sued their asses off.

JAKE: Well, he lost the case because of one thing, only one little fault.

JOE: One little fault! The man doesn't have his legs anymore and you call that a little fault.

JAKE: That's why he lost the case.

GERRY: Why?

JAKE: Well, you see, he didn't have a leg to stand on.

ZULMA: (*From kitchen window.*) You two fell for the old hokey dokey.

GERRY: He was pulling our leg all the time.

JAKE: Just like the doctor's pulled old Rufus' legs off. He didn't have a leg to stand on.

JOE: (*To Zulma.*) Get back to the stove.

ZULMA: What's the matter, you can't stand being taken for a ride.

(Zulma exits to the kitchen.)

JOE: You know that's one of my old routines.

JAKE: Sure, it is. I was surprised you didn't catch on sooner.

JOE: He didn't have a leg to stand on.

GERRY: You wanna hear a new Polish joke?

JAKE: Naw.

JOE: Have you got any nice nigger jokes?

JAKE: a Jewish joke.

ZULMA: *(Entering from kitchen.)* Here's your things, Jake.

JAKE: Thanks baby . . . you know I'm going to come here even more than before. I only come here as a last resort, like when everything else is closed. That's why he's open so late, if it closed any earlier no one would come in here to . . .

JOE: Can it, Jake, can it.

JAKE: Give me a couple'a them donuts.

ZULMA: What kind, we got, jelly . . . chocolate and . . .

JAKE: Two jelly.

JOE: Jake, for you they're seventy-five cents apiece.

JAKE: Seventy-five cents apiece, are you for real?

JOE: Yes and so are the jelly donuts too.

ZULMA: Can't you see it in his baby-brown eyes that he is?

JAKE: Seventy-five cents apiece! That's highway robbery!

JOE: Seventy-five cents, take it or leave it.

JAKE: You got any matches, Joe?

JOE: It's a penny a book.

JAKE: *(Tossing a penny on the counter.)* Here, don't spend it all in one place.

JOE: Thank you . . . and I won't . . . pennies make dollars.

JAKE: So I've heard. *(Zulma exits to pay phone.)*

GERRY: The phone is customers only, Zulma . . . no out calls except on your break and then we would appreciate it if you'd go out and make it on the corner.

ZULMA: What! No calls?

JOE: That's our policy . . . no calls except emergency. *(Zulma exits to the street.)* You got what you wanted, now what else can we serve you?

JAKE: That's what I like about this place, the hospitality that one receives. Makes your eyes want to water with tears . . . just like . . . you know what this place makes me remember . . . the night that I was invited to a great outdoors party by the Ku Klux Klan and I was going to be the guest of honor . . . I always felt guilty

84

that I didn't make that shindig, but you know a man of my importance just can't make every party he's invited to . . .

JOE: I bet they were put off by your absence.

JAKE: Shit, I know they were.

GERRY: Why don't you two cut it out for a little while?

JOE: Cut what out?

JAKE: Cut what out?

GERRY: The bullshit. (*Zulma enters.*)

ZULMA: My sister doesn't answer the phone . . . I get a little worried.

JOE: You wanna go over and see if she needs anything?

ZULMA: Naw . . . you know it's cold out there tonight . . . I couldn't believe it, a two-car accident happened as I walked from here to the phone on the corner. What a place this town is . . . someday, I think I'll leave this town for good, never come back.

GERRY: How many times in your life have you said that?

ZULMA: Since I first got off the train in 1954 . . . I wanted to go right back, but I didn't, I stuck it out to reach the pedestals of failure. I never set out to be a giant in the theatre world or in any world, for that matter, I just wanted to be a part of wherever I was, to be noticed, to be recognized for what I brought to the atmosphere. I never asked anyone to give me for my talent or for any type of work that I put out there from my soul.

JOE: Do we have to go through your life history again?

JAKE: I kinda like listening to life histories.

GERRY: So do I, but once is enough for me.

JOE: You can say that again.

GERRY: So do I, but once is enough for me.

JOE: Really, Gerry, you're getting cornier by the day.

GERRY: It's the sun, Joe . . . the sun ripens me up.

JOE: It does something to you, all right.

JOE: The sun did something to me too.

GERRY: No shit, Sherlock.

JOE: Hey, Zulma, you wanna fix some fresh coffee?

ZULMA: Okay, Joe.

JAKE: Well, I think it's time that I be leaving or else the girls are going to think that the earth swallowed me up.

JOE: Okay! Jake, take care of yourself and give the girls a hello for me.

GERRY: For me, too.

JOE: I knew you'd say that, Gerry.

ZULMA: Oh! So you guys know Jake's girls.

JOE: I don't know them personally, at least I mean, I don't *know them*, but there's someone else here that does!

ZULMA: Who is that?

JOE: (*Imitating various movie villains.*) What you take me for, a squealer . . . a fink . . . a rat . . . a stool pidgeon, I won't talk, that's not my cup of tea . . . I won't talk, but if you look at the person I'll whistle Dixie.

JAKE: Yeah, you'll whistle Dixie all right when you drop in the parlor and see those two blondes.

JOE: Not me!

JAKE: Yep, you and Gerry. Joe, you're no different than any other man who lives alone and needs the companionship that a woman can give. They feel good and you'll feel good and I feel good . . . when people feel good I make money and that makes me feel extra good. You see in a way, it's like a therapy program and I'm Doctor Feelgood . . . I can probably pick up a master's degree on feelgood sometime in some college . . . what do you think, Joe, is there a course in college that trains men and women in my profession, making people feel good, making lonely men who can't seem to find the right kind of talk for a woman feel good, old men who can't make the grade anymore, give them a chance to feel like a man again?

JOE: I know you fifteen years, right?

JAKE: Yeah, fifteen miserable years. Hey, that's a real long time . . .

GERRY: (*Opening the cash register.*) Any more quarters in the box, Joe?

JOE: Naw, you're going to have to go to the bank later on today.

GERRY: Okay, will do.

JOE: Fifteen years, right?

JAKE: Right.

JOE: For fifteen years, just like tonight, you come in here and called me a nigger and you know something, Jake, I don't like it. I don't like it one bit. I don't like being called a nigger by you or any other nigger. Get that straight.

JAKE: I've been called a nigger all my life.

JOE: Well, Jake, I can't help it if you are one. (*Gerry breaks into a roar of laughter. Zulma joins in on the joke. Joe begins to laugh too. Jake starts to laugh. Joe begins to shake, to choke. He lets out a stifled yelp. He falls to the floor.*)

JAKE: Hey man, come on, don't joke like that man, come on man, be cool.

GERRY: Joe, Joe, come on Joe. He's right, don't joke like this.

ZULMA: Joe . . . Joe.

JAKE: Zulu, call the police . . . call an ambulance, hurry . . .

ZULMA: (At phone.) Right . . . Right . . . hello, operator . . . damn it to hell . . .

JAKE: Quick, go out and get a cop.

ZULMA: I'll go. Hold on, Joe, I'll be right back. (Zulma exits.)

GERRY: Oh, Joe, please don't do this, Joe, don't you go and die on me. Joe . . .

JAKE: Joe, Joe, hang in there baby, hang in there, you can beat it.

JOE: Gerry . . . Gerry . . . Gerry!!

GERRY: I'm right here, Joe. I'm right here. I'm not going anywhere. I'm right by your side.

JOE: Oh, Gerry, I thought I would be different.

GERRY: Save your energy, Joe. Don't talk . . .

JOE: Where's that nigger?

JAKE: Joe, baby, be cool man, Gerry's right, save your energy.

JOE: Two big-tit natural blondes, hey?

JAKE: Forget about that, Joe, save your energy man, be cool.

JOE: Two big-tit natural blondes, I bet that's something to see.

JAKE: You'll see them, Joe, you'll see them. I'll bring them around for you.

JOE: Don't look like that, Gerry . . . leave. Gerry . . . go away.

GERRY: What are you talking about, Joe, I'm staying right here with you.

JOE: No . . . no . . . leave, Gerry . . . 'cause I'm leaving soon . . . go away, take a trip.

JAKE: (Crossing to the door.) Where's Zulu with the cop?

JOE: Forget about the cop, you can't ever get one when you need one.

GERRY: Please, Joe, take it easy, everything is going to be all right.

JOE: Jake, tell him about Europe.

JAKE: I don't know anything about Europe.

JOE: Damn it, nigger, you could lie.

JAKE: Yeah, I could lie, Europe is . . .

JOE: Listen to him, Gerry, listen to him and leave this place before it kills you. Oh, look at this. I'm pissing in my pants. Gerry . . . Jake, don't tell anyone about this.

JAKE: Oh, Joe, take it easy, please man.

GERRY: Please, Joe, don't die on me, please Joe, don't leave me alone. I have nobody but you, Joe, please don't . . .

JOE: Gerry . . . Gerry . . . I'm tired of hanging in there . . . Jake . . . look at this, I'm farting my life away . . . I feel like a baby . . .

GERRY: Oh, God, please help him, don't let him die on me, don't take him away from me, please God, please.

JOE: Gerry . . . Gerry . . . I can't think of anything famous to say . . .

(Fade to black.)

Eulogy for a
Small Time Thief

CHARACTERS

DAVID DANCER, *Early thirties*
ROSEMARIE PAULS, *Early thirties*
NICOLE PAULS, *Teenager*
TERRY LOGAN, *Late twenties*
ELAINE (LANEY), *Teenager*
RITA BARKELY, *Teenager*
MILES, Late fifties
CARLOS, *Early twenties*

ACT I

SCENE: *An apartment in north Philadelphia. Most of the play area is the living room, kitchen, and bedroom.*
TIME: *The present.*

(David in bedroom. Rosemarie in kitchen. Entrance to apartment is through kitchen.)

DAVID: Hey, Rosemarie, you know who I ran into today?
ROSEMARIE: What ya say?
DAVID: Flaco, I ran into Flaco today.
ROSEMARIE: Oh yeah, how's he doing?
DAVID: Bad, real bad. He's greasy. I mean real greasy, greasier than a porkchop from a soul shop.
ROSEMARIE: That's too bad. He was such a nice dude.
DAVID: Yeah, he sure was, wasn't he?
ROSEMARIE: Yeah, he was.
DAVID: I also saw Terry Logan down in Center City.
ROSEMARIE: Terry Logan?
DAVID: Yeah, Terry Logan from New York City.
ROSEMARIE: Terry Logan, do I know him?
DAVID: Yeah, you know him. He's the fellow that put us up in Brooklyn.
ROSEMARIE: Oh yeah, I remember him. What's he doing in Philly?
DAVID: Same thing we were doing in New York.
ROSEMARIE: I hope you invited him over if he needs a place to stay.
DAVID: Naw, he has a place in the south side, but I told him to come over if he wanted to party sometime.
ROSEMARIE: That's nice. We owe him a solid.
DAVID: That's what I figured you say, so I told him to drop over tonight.
ROSEMARIE: Tonight?
DAVID: Yeah, tonight.
ROSEMARIE: Oh, that's right. We have Nicole coming over with some friends, right?
DAVID: Right.
ROSEMARIE: What time you tell him to come by?
DAVID: Any time after 8.
ROSEMARIE: That's cool.

DAVID: Hey, have you seen my light blue pants?

ROSEMARIE: They're in the cleaners. I dropped them off this morning while you were asleep. The telephone man came by, too.

DAVID: He fix the damn thing?

ROSEMARIE: Yeah, a cross wire or something was wrong with it. I really don't remember what he said was wrong with it . . .

DAVID: Do I got any clean socks around?

ROSEMARIE: In the bag on the sofa.

DAVID: (David enters living room). I see it . . .

ROSEMARIE: Bring the bag in here

DAVID: Here catch. (Throws bag.) Here are my old smelly socks. Put them under your pillow for safekeeping. (He comes out of room, attacks her with a pillow. She runs into bedroom. Grabs a pillow. A friendly pillow fight ensues.)

DAVID: Hey, Baby, let's fuck before your sister arrives.

ROSEMARIE: Come on . . . (They run into the bedroom. The doorbell rings.)

DAVID: Aw shit, goddamn it . . . Hey, Nicole, how's your whatyamacollit?

NICOLE: My whatyamacollit is all right, and her whatyamacollit is all right too and, by the way, whatyamacollit's name is Fenders . . . and he's a nice guy whatyamacallit.

DAVID: Okay, okay, you don't have to bite my head off what-yamacallit.

ROSEMARIE: Leave my man's head alone, find your own head to bite on.

NICOLE: Hi, Baby, how you been? . . . This gorilla treating you like a queen?

ROSEMARIE: If he don't, I'll be long gone.

DAVID: Door's open.

ROSEMARIE: If I took that seriously, I'd hit the streets in a hot second.

DAVID: Like I said, the door is open. You can book out of here anytime you want, girl . . . if you can walk with a broken leg.

NICOLE: I'll carry her out.

DAVID: With your arms in a sling, that's a good trick if you can pull it off.

NICOLE: What you got for the head beside a comb?

ROSEMARIE: There's some smoke in the jar over by the set . . .

DAVID: There's some beer in the frig . . . and rum in the cabinet . . .

NICOLE: Well, all right . . . lead me to some smoke . . .

ROSEMARIE: You got to roll it yourself.

NICOLE: No big problem there, honey.

ROSEMARIE: I gather that much just by the stains on your fingers.

NICOLE: That's a little problem I've been trying to get rid of.

ROSEMARIE: I have something for that, honey. Come in here.

NICOLE: You know after a while the reefer really stains your fingers bad. (*The phone rings as Nicole exits into kitchen.*)

DAVID: I hear . . . hello . . . oh hi . . . so what's happening with the coke. Nothing huh . . . shit, that's bad . . . naw I was counting on doing up some blow tonight . . . yeah I got a friend dropping by tonight . . . no, a guy I know from the big apple . . . no, really a guy . . . I . . . oh, fuck you, man . . . so how's the kids? . . . that's good . . . and Sheila . . . she got over that cold? Oh good . . . well, tell her I said hello . . . yeah . . . okay, and give my best to the kids too . . . yeah, I'm gonna come out and see them soon . . . no, nothing special . . . If you want to drop by later tonight, do so, okay . . . then I see you tomorrow at work . . . No, everything is still go for the thing tomorrow morning . . . Have a nice sleep, okay, okay, bye . . . Catch you later. That was Brains on the phone . . . He said nothing is happening with the snow. . . . All he got is monster left . . . what . . . I hate speed.

ROSEMARIE: I said that Nicole brought some with her . . .

DAVID: Coke?

ROSEMARIE: No, her kotexes.

DAVID: Shit, I'll sniff them up, too . . . the way that sister of yours is looking these days . . . they'll give me a . . .

ROSEMARIE: Oh, shut up . . . you . . . you pre-vert . . . she's only sixteen.

DAVID: Ripe as a melon.

NICOLE: Here, I only have a little bit of C left but it's yours.

DAVID: A little bit from Nicole . . . thank you.

ROSEMARIE: You're quite welcome.

DAVID: Come 'ere girl . . .

ROSEMARIE: Get away from me, you degenerate . . .

DAVID: Come 'ere , sugar, share some of this with me.

ROSEMARIE: No thank you.

DAVID: You don't want none really?

ROSEMARIE: No, there's not enough for the both of us . . . so you take it yourself.

DAVID: Isn't this something, sacrificing like that . . .

NICOLE: Above and beyond the call of duty.

ROSEMARIE: Yes, all that, and also I already had some in the bathroom.

DAVID: Oh, shit, you had me believing all that crap . . . you spoil a wet dream.

NICOLE: The crowning glory of his life has been a wet dream . . .

DAVID: High school wise-ass . . . but not a bad-looking ass at that . . .

ROSEMARIE: Back, boy . . . back.

NICOLE: You're too old for me . . .

DAVID: Don't you believe in a second childhood?

NICOLE: Yeah, but not for you . . . you haven't even reached adulthood yet . . .

DAVID: Sit on this and rotate.

NICOLE: I would if I could, I can't so I won't . . .

DAVID: Hey, by the way, how's your brother doing? Rosemarie told me this morning you was going to drop off and see him today at the hospital.

NICOLE: He's coming along pretty well, considering they can't take out the bullet yet. . . . It dug deep in the brain. Doctor says he may lose his eyesight.

DAVID: Well, he did it to himself, you know. I mean like I told him that guy in the store was pretty hard up for money. You saw that big-ass dog he keeps in the place . . . the one your brother killed in the holdup, that was a mean-ass dog, almost torn your brother's stomach open, didn't he? . . . yep, bad-ass dog, kept mean and vicious by a money-starved man. . . . Bad business, bad business . . . you know we been setting up this A & P for about three weeks now, right? . . . and Pan was suppose to be in on it . . . a much safer job than those small stores on the avenue, I mean these storekeepers are doing about as bad as we are in these times, right? And the people that work for them now-a-days take their position very serious, sometimes you got to whip them up a little before they give in . . . times are changing for the worst. . . . There was a time when a man could go into a store, pull out his roscoe, take the money and split . . . no trouble, no hassle, no big thing. . . . Now, today you got to beat them over the head or shoot them in the leg or something violent like that, you know what I mean? . . . This business is getting more and more hazardous as the years go by, you know. It's the government that's to blame for all this . . . violent crimes . . . and Hollywood, too. I mean all these dumb movies about men and women taking the law into their own hands, karate this and kung-fu that . . . why do you think I gave up the mugging business? . . . cause everytime you pulled a blade on someone, they been taking up karate lessons in some rip-off place . . . I mean a jerk learns a couple of self-defense moves and already he thinks he's Bruce Lee's second cousin, so you end up stabbing the poor idiot in self defense. Then if you get busted, it's no longer a simple mugging, no it's attempted murder with a felony to boot. . . . Can't wait to get the hell out of the business . . . there's no compensation that goes along with the job, no medi-care, no Blue Cross or Red Cross, there's no crosses at all except the ones we put ourselves into . . . there's two many informers out there . . . there's too many prisons, too many cops, not enough professional people in the streets, all these novices robbing people. I know a guy, a friend of mines, right, cases this liquor store for three days . . . he has everything set . . . what happens as he is in the store, preparing himself to make the hit . . . these two teenage kids come in with shotguns, announce a stickup, they get nervous, uptight, and they blow the manager away and blew my friend's leg off, very unprofessional, no talent whatsoever . . . anyway, he got to waste one of them as they left the store, but then he was booked on carrying a concealed, unregistered weapon and involuntary man-slaughter . . . they threw the case out of court but gave him six months on the weapons charge . . . him being on parole had to go back on a violation for another six months, so he ends up doing a year . . . all that and, you know what, these kids got away with guess . . . fifty-six dollars . . . really ridiculous. Now John is on welfare, taking the city's handout, a nice independent man like him on welfare . . . it's a crying shame . . . a real shame . . . but those are the breaks of life . . . but I got things pretty well down pat for my move out of this place . . . these next two jobs should wheel me in enough bread to retire to a nice place in South America . . . yep, gonna be a farmer out in South America, gonna grow marijuana and import cocaine . . . I think things are gonna work out for the best in the end of this chapter of my life . . . but I am really sorry about Pan, though, I mean he's a great wheelman, stupid of him to carry a gun . . . should have stuck to his own thing, but like I say, it's a small-time thief's fate to hit upon someone who's been taking karate lessons . . .

NICOLE: Those are the breaks of life.

DAVID: Those *are* the breaks of life.

ROSEMARIE: You want a beer, Baby?

DAVID: No thanks, Honey.

ROSEMARIE: How about you, Nicole?

NICOLE: Not now, thanks.

ROSEMARIE: Well, I'm getting one, and I am not sharing with anyone.

DAVID: Capitalist.

NICOLE: Imperialist.

ROSEMARIE: Don't forget warmonger.

NICOLE and DAVID: Warmonger.

ROSEMARIE: You see, that always works. I feel guilty as all hell. (Enters kitchen.)

NICOLE: Did you tell her yet?

DAVID: No, not yet.

NICOLE: When?

DAVID: Soon, baby, soon.

NICOLE: How soon?

DAVID: Real soon, don't worry.

ROSEMARIE: (From kitchen.) You want a rum and coke, anybody?

DAVID: Yeah, I do.

NICOLE: Me, too, I'll have one, too . . . make it sooner than that.

DAVID: Don't threaten me, baby, I don't like that.

NICOLE: It's not a threat.

DAVID: Just so you know where I stand, I don't like being bossed around by anyone at all, you get me?

NICOLE: It's not a threat. I went to the doctor this morning. That's why I told Rosemarie I went to see Panama at the hospital . . .

DAVID: You went to the doctor, for what?

NICOLE: I missed my period this month.

DAVID: So what, you might get a double period at the end of next month.

NICOLE: Be serious.

DAVID: Okay, I'm serious, now what?

ROSEMARIE: You're serious about what?

DAVID: Oh . . . hmm . . . about leaving the business forever, moving out to South America.

ROSEMARIE: Oh, he's serious about that all right, we already got passports.

NICOLE: Passports?

ROSEMARIE: Yes, dearie, you can't get out the country without them.

NICOLE: You didn't say anything about passports.

DAVID: I figure you would figure that out yourself, baby.

NICOLE: I'm beginning to.

ROSEMARIE: What's the matter, baby?

NICOLE: Nothing, Rosemarie, just that it took me by surprise, that's all.

ROSEMARIE: Oh, don't worry about it . . . we'll be coming back now and then.

DAVID: Yeah, we will . . .

NICOLE: I bet you will.

ROSEMARIE: Aw, she's feeling rejected.

NICOLE: In more ways than one.

DAVID: Well, you shouldn't . . . you know what they say about the best laid plans . . .

NICOLE: No, I don't.

DAVID: Read about it . . .

NICOLE: When I get to college.

ROSEMARIE: Pull in your claws, honey.

NICOLE: I'm sorry, it just that, well, I guess you know what I mean.

ROSEMARIE: We do, Baby . . . but we'll send for you during summer vacations.

DAVID: Sure we will . . . look, let's get off this subject, okay?

ROSEMARIE: Sure.

DAVID: Nicole . . .

NICOLE: Yeah, I'm getting bored with it.

DAVID: I already feel that way.

ROSEMARIE: Good.

DAVID: Okay. These two that you got coming today, what you know of them?

NICOLE: They need some bread to get some things that they can't afford. They told their parents that they were going to sit tonight, that they'd be a little late, if you know what I mean . . .

DAVID: Next, you'll be curling up your moustache, Dasterly Dan.

ROSEMARIE: Come on, David, drop it.

DAVID: Did you break it down for them as far as dollars and cents goes?

NICOLE: Course.

DAVID: Last time those two little money hungry friends of yours gave me a real hard time . . . you know I really don't need to do this shit, I only do it so that you can get a couple of bucks in your pocketbook.

96

NICOLE: I heard you run the same story over and over again, and I still don't buy it . . .

DAVID: You really don't believe me, that I don't need to be doing this shit?

ROSEMARIE: Of course, she believes you.

DAVID: No, no, let's get this here thing straightened out right now. You think that I need to take the chances of being arrested.

NICOLE: Well, if you need it or not, you're taking the chances, right?

DAVID: This is it . . . David Dancer, this is it . . . after today, no more of this penny-ante pimp routine for you, not in your house, baby.

ROSEMARIE: David, please, don't fly off the handle like that, baby.

DAVID: Don't fly off the what . . .

ROSEMARIE: Baby, please, your blood pressure . . .

DAVID: Did you hear what came out of this young girl's mouth? . . . she really thinks we need this shit to survive . . .

NICOLE: I didn't say that you did.

DAVID: If I hadn't said it, you would have.

NICOLE: You'll never know that now, will you?

DAVID: That's it . . . this is it, no more after today . . . you and your little friends are going to have to find another place to make your babysitting money . . . the nerve of this woman to think that I David Dancer need a sixteen-year-old girl to help get over . . . I was . . . no, I ain't going to get into the way I walked barefoot to school routine with you 'cause you wouldn't believe it either . . . the phone, Rosemarie . . .

ROSEMARIE: Okay, I hear it, you don't have to shout.

DAVID: Sorry, baby . . . who is it . . .

ROSEMARIE: Wrong number.

DAVID: Wrong number.

ROSEMARIE: Wrong number . . . haven't you ever heard of a wrong number?

DAVID: David Dancer never gets a wrong number.

ROSEMARIE: Well, you got one now.

DAVID: Next time I'll answer the phone, and you'll see that I never, in all the years that I have had a phone, have never not once ever have I received a wrong number. (*Nicole gets up, does an up-tempo marching song. Her voice acting as instruments.*)

NICOLE: America, you have had another first. David Dancer has received his first wrong number.

ROSEMARIE: Nicole, calm down.

DAVID: You see what I mean, she doesn't believe anything I say. She's always calling me a liar in a direct or indirect way.

ROSEMARIE: Well, she is a little skeptic, runs in the family.

DAVID: A little skeptic.

NICOLE: Skeptics run in the family.

DAVID: You know what's going to run in the family pretty soon is broken jaws and missing front teeth.

ROSEMARIE: Well, we're not exactly twins, you know.

NICOLE: Copping out on me, huh?

ROSEMARIE: Well, to put it mildly, yes.

DAVID: Skeptic, that's a good one.

NICOLE: Can't wait to hear what happens when you receive your first obscene phone call. You should get in touch with the world book of records.

DAVID: You're a regular riot, girl.

ROSEMARIE: You guys act like a . . . couple . . . of lovers . . .

DAVID: What did you say . . . come on, speak up . . .

ROSEMARIE: Nothing . . . it's nothing . . . I was speaking to myself.

DAVID: That's all right to speak to yourself, but when you start answering yourself, that's when you should start thinking about seeing someone for help.

NICOLE: Oh, Johnny Carson will just love you.

DAVID: As much as you do.

NICOLE: Maybe a little less.

ROSEMARIE: Let's set up the place. These people should be arriving soon.

NICOLE: Who's coming for my girls?

DAVID: They're all right, two hicks . . .

NICOLE: Do they want to make a scene of it?

DAVID: Naw, I don't think so . . . you know, very macho and shit uptight.

NICOLE: Factory workers again.

DAVID: They got a little bread.

NICOLE: That's just it, they have a little bread, not much more than a little.

DAVID: Maybe you should start your own recruiting service, too.

NICOLE: There's no maybe about that, Mr. David Dancer.

ROSEMARIE: How many joints should we roll up?

DAVID: About ten should do it.

NICOLE: Are you charging for the joints again, Mr. David Dancer.

DAVID: Yes, I am young lady, that's ten dollars that we can use to buy toilet paper. The way you run your mouth off, anyone would think you have diarrhea in your tonsils.

NICOLE: Funny . . . oh my, you're so funny . . . who open the door to your cage?

DAVID: The heat between your legs melted the steel bars like butter.

ROSEMARIE: I'm going into the kitchen to roll, you want to help me, Nicole?

DAVID: She can't help herself, she going to help you?

ROSEMARIE: Coming?

NICOLE: Yeah, yeah, I'm coming . . . hold your horses.

DAVID: Hurry, hurry, step right up and see the youngest madame in town.

NICOLE: Are you going to tell her?

DAVID: Not now . . .

NICOLE: If you don't, I will.

DAVID: You will what?

NICOLE: Tell her about us.

DAVID: Go on, tell her . . . no one is stopping you, go on hurry up, tell her.

NICOLE: Go the hell.

DAVID: Meet you there . . . and by the way, keep a clean sheet for me . . .

NICOLE: I will.

DAVID: Thank you, I won't forget you for that . . .

NICOLE: I'll try to remain in your graces.

DAVID: Well, you should, I have a lot of pull down there. You know me, Chip Ricsaw, the devil's brother-in-law . . .

NICOLE: Now what about these proletarians you're throwing on me today?

DAVID: Well, I met them at the bar across the street. They work in the same factory over on the west side of town . . . been in the city not too long. The come from, let me see where do they come from? . . . I'm not really sure, but I guess we can ask them when they get here if you're really that interested . . .

NICOLE: I'm not really that interested in where they come from.

DAVID: Just on whether they come.

NICOLE: Funny.

DAVID: Just couldn't resist it, you left yourself so wide open for that.

NICOLE: Well, try to control yourself, okay?

DAVID: Check . . . you got it, kid.

NICOLE: Now go over their history one more time, but keep it straight.

DAVID: Well, okay . . . the guy with the moustache, his name is Carlos or Carlo . . . didn't have time to check out whether it was his first name or his last . . . don't really matter anyway . . . he's like a foreman or something like that at this place where they work at . . . the younger, his name is Robert Gel-something or other, he just kinda moved in last month . . . he's not married, and they're really both as horny as a couple of mutts in heat . . . the older guy Carlos or Carlo, he sort of takes the job of running the kid's social life, kinda like a big brother, you know what I mean . . . he's into a very heavy gangster type of trip with the kid, ought to be easy bait for you . . . so we have to play the role of a heavy operation in the making when he gets here.

NICOLE: You ain't taking me alive, copper . . . come and get me . . .

DAVID: Yeah, that's just the shit he believes in, you know what I mean . . . I met them at the bar, we shared a few drinks, a few half-hearted laughs, then I invited them over for a hand of poker with the elbow in the rib type of hint. I practically had to hit them over the head with what I really meant . . . anyway, the foreman Carlos agrees to come over. . . . He wanted to know if there would be any broads around . . . well, by the time I finished describing you, the kid Robert came in his pants. Hey, by the way, these friends of yours, they look all right, I mean they don't have . . .

NICOLE: The claps?

DAVID: Shit, I don't give a damn if they have the claps or not, all I'm interested in is if they look good, and by the way, they are not interested in any black women, they wan some fat juicy white thighs crushing them to death.

NICOLE: They call that projection.

DAVID: I thought you said we would keep it straight.

NICOLE: Just couldn't resist it, you left yourself wide open.

DAVID: Okay, we're even.

NICOLE: You know what they say, pay back is a bitch.

DAVID: Okay, everybody knows that we must keep a united front. The role for tonight is big-time action. Rosemarie, you're Ma Baker, and I'm Al Capone.

NICOLE: How about me . . . Bonnie Parker?

DAVID: No, Xavier Hollander would be better.

ROSEMARIE: Typecasted again, Nicole.

100

NICOLE: You're siding with him.

DAVID: She is my old lady.

NICOLE: And she is my sister.

ROSEMARIE: Mostly I'm me . . . Rosemarie Pauls.

DAVID: What did you promise the girls?

NICOLE: Fifty.

DAVID: A piece?

NICOLE: Yes, a piece.

DAVID: Nicole, these guys are coming here to rent a piece of pussy, not to buy it . . .

ROSEMARIE: That's the door, I'll get it.

NICOLE: Fifty is what I said, and fifty is what it'll be or forget it.

DAVID: Okay, no hassles, I just wonder what you're getting.

NICOLE: None of your business . . . all you need to know is that I get twenty percent of what you make here tonight. Do you have any idea on what that'll be?

ROSEMARIE: Your friends are here, Nicole.

NICOLE: Oh, hello . . . David Dancer meet Rita and Laney . . .

DAVID: Hi, girls . . .

RITA: Hello, Mr. Dancer.

DAVID: Naw, just call me David.

ELAINE: Hello, David.

DAVID: Sit down, make yourself comfortable.

ROSEMARIE: Can I get you girls something?

RITA: No, thank you. I don't drink.

ELAINE: Me neither.

DAVID: You smoke . . . pot, that is.

ELAINE: No, thanks, I don't smoke.

RITA: Neither do I.

DAVID: Shit . . . you wanna play parchisi? . . .

ROSEMARIE: Spin the bottle?

NICOLE: They're just goofing on, you pay them no mind, after a while you become immune to their insults and insanity.

DAVID: Your dates should be here soon.

ROSEMARIE: You take coke?

RITA: No.

ROSEMARIE: Speed?

ELAINE: No.

DAVID: Uppers?

RITA: NO.

ROSEMARIE: Downers?

ELAINE: No.

DAVID: Do you take church on Sundays?

RITA: Do we what?

DAVID: You know, take the piece of bread on Sundays?

ELAINE: Yes.

DAVID: You do?

RITA: Yes.

ROSEMARIE: Do you live with your parents?

ELAINE: What is this, a quiz show?.

RITA: Yeah, Nicole, I thought you said we was going to a hip place, get high, lay a couple of guys and split with a few bucks in our wallet. If I knew I had to give a case history on my life, I would have said . . .

DAVID: No . . . no . . . hold up a second, don't get us wrong, baby.

RITA: We ain't getting you wrong, you're making yourself wrong.

ELAINE: Yeah man, we don't need all this shit.

DAVID: Sorry . . . it's just that the other friends of Nicole . . .

ELAINE: We're not the other friends of Nicole, we are these friends, right here not before nor after . . .

RITA: Be here now . . . or don't be at all . . .

ELAINE: Check it out, baby.

DAVID: You don't have to beat me with a wet mop to get the point, baby.

ELAINE: We sure hope so.

RITA: Yes, that could be very boring after the second whipping.

DAVID: Oh yeah, Nicole, what we were discussing before I say about five yards . . .

NICOLE: Chump change . . .

DAVID: That's what some people call it, but I'm not those in need.

RITA: Can we choose or is this set up already?

NICOLE: I don't know, ask David.

ELAINE: Well . . .

DAVID: Well what?

RITA: Can we choose or this thing set up?

DAVID: No, choose within yourselves.

RITA: Is this a regular thing with yous?

ROSEMARIE: What is this, we're taking turns on interrogation.

DAVID: No, just a side thing.

ELAINE: What do you usually do?

ROSEMARIE: Not much of anything, to be truthful.

DAVID: We get over.

RITA: Oh, I see, this is your office.

ELAINE: Actually, they have a great estate in the country.

NICOLE: No, but they do have a nice farm.

ROSEMARIE: One hundred and five acres of good farming land.

DAVID: Yep, in a few months, we'll be living on it permanently.

ELAINE: Really . . .

DAVID: Yep, always wanted to say yep like that, you know, yep, always had a secret longing to be a farmer.

NICOLE: Well, soon your dream will be true.

DAVID: You ain't lying.

ELAINE: I think that's nice.

DAVID: Yeah, we think so . . . yep, we sure think so, yep we sure do.

ELAINE: You're really going to get it off, huh, all that yep shit?

DAVID: Yep, as much as possible. Every chance that I get to say yep, I'm going to say it . . . yep, I sure am, yep.

RITA: Yep, you sure are, ain't you?

DAVID: Yep, I sure am.

ELAINE: That's nice, but it's also boring.

DAVID: Yep, it sure is, sometimes . . . yep, sure is boring.

ROSEMARIE: Yep.

NICOLE: Yep.

RITA: Yep.

ELAINE: Yep.

DAVID: Yep.

ROSEMARIE: Yep.

NICOLE: Yep.

RITA: Yep, yep.

ELAINE: Yep, yep, yep.

DAVID: Yep, yep, yep, yep.

ROSEMARIE: Yep, yep, yep, yep, yep, yep, yep, yep, yep, yep, yep, yep, yep, yep.

DAVID: Door, someone's at the door.

ROSEMARIE: Yep, that what it sounds like, sounds like someone's at the door.

DAVID: Well . . .

ROSEMARIE: Well what?

DAVID: Well, ain't you gonna answer the door?

ROSEMARIE: No.

DAVID: No?

ROSEMARIE: No.

DAVID: No.

ELAINE: Seem that's what she said first.

RITA: Yep, I heard her say it first, she said no first.

NICOLE: So did I.

DAVID: Are you going to let whoever is knocking wait out there?

ROSEMARIE: Yep.

DAVID: You are?

ROSEMARIE: Yep.

DAVID: Why?

ROSEMARIE: Because you heard the knocking first, why didn't you get up and answer it?

DAVID: Because I asked you.

ROSEMARIE: No, you didn't ask me.

DAVID: I didn't?

ROSEMARIE: No, you didn't.

DAVID: Then what did I do?

ROSEMARIE: You ordered.

DAVID: I ordered?

ROSEMARIE: Yes, you ordered. Am I right, girls?

ELAINE: So it seems.

RITA: I think that's what he did.

NICOLE: I'm sure that's what he did.

ROSEMARIE: You see, that's what you did.

DAVID: I did not.

ROSEMARIE: Yes, you did.

ELAINE: Yep.

RITA: Yep.

NICOLE: Yep.

DAVID: Oh, let's not go over that routine again.

ROSEMARIE: Yep, let's not go over it again.

DAVID: I'll answer the door, will that satisfy you?

ROSEMARIE: No, but it will satisfy whoever is knocking out there.

NICOLE: I think it will.

ELAINE: I know it would satisfy me if I was knocking on the door.

RITA: Me too.

DAVID: You girls get together, and a man ain't got a chance.

ROSEMARIE: Sure you do, you got the chance to answer the door, isn't that wonderful?

DAVID: Oh, I'm thrilled to the marrow.

ROSEMARIE: You see, it's already in your bones.

NICOLE: Let it go a little longer, and it'll get into your soul.

DAVID: Thanks.

104

NICOLE: Don't mention it, it's nothin'.

DAVID: I agree with that . . . and neither are you.

ROSEMARIE: Foul.

ELAINE: Foul.

RITA: Foul.

NICOLE: Foul.

DAVID: Yep, it is, isn't it?

NICOLE: That's your speed anyway.

DAVID: Well, I needed something to protect myself.

ROSEMARIE: A big handsome man like you.

DAVID: Flattery will get you nowhere. Who is it? Who? Hey, hey, hey, what ya say . . . Hey, honey, it's Terry. Terry Logan from Brooklyn, come on in, man, come on in. I thought you was going to get here at a later hour.

TERRY: I was, but being stuck in that hotel gets on my nerves too hard, you know what I mean, man . . .

DAVID: I sure do, I sure do . . . Honey, you remember Terry Logan?

ROSEMARIE: Sure I do, how have you been?

TERRY: Struggling to stay above the water.

ROSEMARIE: Ain't we all?

DAVID: This is Nicole, my old lady's little sister.

ROSEMARIE: Her younger sister.

DAVID: Excuse me, her younger sister.

TERRY: How do you do, David's old lady's younger sister?

NICOLE: Trying to stay above the water.

DAVID: This is her friends, Laney and Rita . . .

TERRY: Hey, how's things, Laney and Rita?

ELAINE: If things are okay with you, they're okay with us.

RITA: My sentiments exactly.

TERRY: Well, what are you people doing today?

DAVID: Nothing much, going to make a few dollars for the ladies.

TERRY: For or on them?

DAVID: A little bit of both, you know what I mean.

TERRY: I sure do.

ROSEMARIE: Would you like something to drink?

TERRY: Sure, you have any herb?

NICOLE: Yeah, but you have to roll your own.

TERRY: No problem there, honey, been doing that since I was nine.

NICOLE: Really, how interesting.

TERRY: No, not really.

NICOLE: I agree with that, too.

TERRY: Did I enter at a wrong time?

DAVID: No, man, we're just sitting here getting on each other's cases.

TERRY: That's nice, don't include me in that okay, I can't stand the dozens.

DAVID: No, we're not playing them any more.

TERRY: Thanks.

ROSEMARIE: Rum and coke, good for the heart.

TERRY: And the head.

DAVID: Yep.

ELAINE: So, you're from New York?

TERRY: No, from Brooklyn.

RITA: Isn't Brooklyn a part of New York?

TERRY: No, New York is part of Brooklyn.

RITA: Really?

ELAINE: No, stupid, that's just his way of thinking.

TERRY: No, that's not my way of thinking, that's the way four million people who live in Brooklyn think. I just go along with their train of philosophy about the city.

ELAINE: Do you go to other parts of New York, too?

TERRY: Sometimes, when it's necessary I do it. I go to Gunsmoke.

ELAINE: Gunsmoke?

DAVID: That's a nickname for Brooklyn.

RITA: Really, that's cute, Gunsmoke. Why do they call it Gunsmoke.

TERRY: Because guns seem to smoke when they are triggered into firing.

RITA: So what does it all mean?

DAVID: It means that in Brooklyn, there's a lot of guns being fired.

TERRY: It's a hold over from the fifties.

DAVID: More like the twenties, if you ask me.

ROSEMARIE: I don't remember anyone asking.

DAVID: That's just in case, anyway let's drop this playing for a while.

ROSEMARIE: Who's playing?

DAVID: I'm serious.

ROSEMARIE: Okay, baby, anything you say.

DAVID: Don't make me repeat myself, Rosemarie.

ROSEMARIE: I won't.

DAVID: Make sure that you don't.

ELAINE: Here, let me light that joint up for you.

TERRY: If you insist.

DAVID: So the city is getting a little hot.

106

TERRY: Like a bonfire, my man, things are not jumping off right in a lot of gigs, you know what I mean, like there's a rat in every corner nowadays, seem like the police are spending a fortune keeping these guys coming up with new potential jobs too hot this summer, so I decided to come out for awhile, see what I can see out here.

DAVID: Tell you the truth, if you picked this city, you're making a mistake. Ain't nothing here but cops on horses with big guns, itching to pull them triggers on the first businessman they come across, really a lot of rookies wearing pistols, that's why I choose to cool it for awhile.

TERRY: Well, with the money you made off with in Brooklyn, I thought by now you be living on easy street.

DAVID: Naw, that was just to pay up a lot of bills. I was operating in the red for a while, now I am even with about everybody I know who I owed money to. Pretty soon in a month or so, I'll be gone.

TERRY: Gone?

DAVID: Yep, gone for a long ass time.

TERRY: Jail.

DAVID: No man, gone. Like away from the city, this city and every other city that I've ever visited or lived in. I mean, I'm getting out of this business and out of the city life.

TERRY: What are you going to do, become a farmer?

DAVID: Hey, how did you know?

TERRY: No man, really? What are you planning on doing?

DAVID: Become a farmer.

TERRY: No, seriously.

DAVID: I am serious.

ROSEMARIE: He is serious. We bought a farm in Maine, and we're heading that way in about six months or so if things work out according to schedule.

TERRY: Really? You really mean it . . . shit, you're really serious.

DAVID: Yeah man, I'm really serious.

NICOLE: Isn't that a dead case?

TERRY: That's really strange. Whatever made you wanna be a farmer?

DAVID: You know, I've never been inside.

TERRY: Never?

DAVID: Well, once as a kid, I was in a youth camp for delinquents. It was on a farm and I used to do all the chores around the place. I was the only kid from the city who liked to do farm work. . . .

Well, the rest of the guys, all thought that I was just bucking to get off the place for good behavior, but I would tell them that I was serious, that I liked getting up at the crack of dawn and being out there with all them animals and, well, they all thought that I was crazy or a rat and when the time came that I was going to leave the place, I asked to stay on but they wouldn't let me so I left and got into the business, stay clear of prison though, couldn't stand being locked up, really not the greatest experience in the world, you know . . . so anyway, I vowed that someday before I died that I would die in a farm out there with nature, not here in the cold metal coffin that we call the city life. This shit is for suckers not for me.

TERRY: Well, I wouldn't go as far as to say that city life is for suckers.

DAVID: Well, what have you got out there in the wonderful city?

TERRY: There is something for those that want to get it.

DAVID: Like what?

TERRY: Well, like whatever you want to get.

DAVID: You see, I agree with that . . . in the city you got a chance to get what you want, but is it what you need . . . I don't think so.

TERRY: Well, if I go after something that I want, it's because I also need whatever that thing is that I want.

DAVID: The city is a river of pollution which pollutes people making it harder to live in it, people like myself and people like you and the rest of the crowd that we know. Man, that ain't a way to enjoy the few years that we have on this planet, especially if you want to leave something behind that said that you lived. A farm, you leave a place where life is growing all the time, where life is never a stalemate. Here life is one coffin-like house to another. Man, that's not for me, no sir, I can't allow my kid to grow up the way I did. I want something special for him, for myself as well, like right now I make a few dollars to survive with while the rest goes into the farm that we bought. 'Cause when I move in I want, I need that place to be mine totally, not just a rental space that I occupy. That what you got in the city, after a while they'll be renting out coffins . . . not me . . . I want to be buried in a place that I know is totally mine, that's why I'm getting out once and for all, it'll be goodbye cruel city, goodbye.

TERRY: Well, to each his own, as the saying goes.

DAVID: Well, look I have these two tricks coming up for the young ladies here.

TERRY: Really, well that leaves me out of the ballpark.

NICOLE: If you're playing in that park.

TERRY: You mean, there's another position open.

TERRY: I'll say there is . . .

TERRY: Well . . . well . . . that's nice to know.

DAVID: Man, they'll melt down the key.

TERRY: Oh, she doesn't look that dangerous to me.

DAVID: You know what they say about looks.

TERRY: I sure do, and I like what I am looking at.

NICOLE: Oh, you're just jealous.

DAVID: The field is open, my man, have fun.

TERRY: That's up to the other player.

NICOLE: Fun is the name of the game.

TERRY: Why don't we go out somewhere?

NICOLE: I'd love to after the business is taken care of first.

TERRY: Business before pleasure, I always say.

NICOLE: That's a good motto, a little old-fashioned, but still good.

TERRY: It has its merits.

SCENE TWO: A *hallway* to *the entrance of David Dancer's home.*

CARLOS: Is this the place?

MILES: Yeah, this is the address and this is the floor and this is the number on the door, so I guess this is the place.

CARLOS: Are you ready?

MILES: I was born ready.

CARLOS: You knock.

MILES: Why . . . can't you knock?

CARLOS: Well, you know how it is.

MILES: No, I don't know how it is.

CARLOS: Come on man, don't be like that.

MILES: Okay, just kidding with you . . . sure I know how it is . . . you know what this reminds me of? . . .

CARLOS: No.

MILES: I never told you this, but I had a son who, if he had lived, would've been around your age now . . . How do you feel?

CARLOS: A little drunk.

MILES: So am I.

CARLOS: Really.

MILES: Sure.

CARLOS: I thought you never got drunk.

109

MILES: Sure, we all do, why not?

CARLOS: I just thought that you never did.

MILES: Oh sure, I get drunk, it's just that I know how to handle my liquor.

CARLOS: Yeah, I can tell.

MILES: Well, you know some men don't know how to.

CARLOS: Oh, I know that.

MILES: Handling your liquor is one of the great secrets of life.

CARLOS: It is.

MILES: It sure is.

CARLOS: How am I doing?

MILES: Not bad, you can do better if you put your mind to it.

CARLOS: Really.

MILES: Sure, it's all up here, all up here, that's where the answer lies.

CARLOS: You sure know a lot.

MILES: Naw, I know about as much as any man who has had the same experience as me.

CARLOS: That's not many.

MILES: Oh, don't say that. There's a lot of men out there in this world have walk similar paths, not many that's true, but enough so that life doesn't become boring with the same routine year after year, like it was out on the farm.

CARLOS: Oh, you lived on a farm . . . sure did a lot for you, huh?

MILES: Well, I guess it had its ups as well as its downers.

CARLOS: And you left?

MILES: Yeah, came out to the city to make my fortune and fame.

CARLOS: You did?

MILES: Yep . . . but I never met either one, fortune or fame, just plain obscurity.

CARLOS: That's not true, I think you're great.

MILES: You're just one man.

CARLOS: Do you need more than one?

MILES: No, no, I don't need more than one.

CARLOS: Should I knock?

MILES: Naw, sit down first . . .

CARLOS: You wanna drink?

MILES: Sure why not . . . you know, you remind me of my son so much. He was as strong and as smart as you. He had curly hair too. He enlisted in the Marine at the age of seventeen. By the time he was twenty he was dead in some rice paddy, step on a

110

booby trap. He was going to be a somebody once he was out. He was a lot like me, he wanted adventure, something I never really went after. No, after a while, I just settle myself to live one day at a time, trying to make happy days to remember in my old age. . . . My daughter, you got to meet my youngest girl, just like her mother she looks like, only she nothing like her in spirit or in thought, she truly independent of anyone just like you, just like my son, just like I always wanted to be like but never could quite capture that attitude. But you can't say I didn't try, no, you can't say I didn't try. I did everything that I ever heard of or thought of or had the courage to do and those things that I feared to do, those where the things that I did first, everything that I was afraid of doing, got to make a stab at it, that what I felt. I had to do, make a stab at all those things that you are afraid of doing than the thing that you wanna do. Do those things last 'cause the things that you wanna do will always be there to be done . . .

CARLOS: When I go out to places with you, I somehow feel so much like a child who is near a mighty oak tree of learning.

MILES: Strange, I get the same kind of feeling with you. I feel much older, not older in age but older in all the knowledge that I've acquired during my years on this good earth of ours . . .

CARLOS: Yeah, that's strange, seems like we were meant to have been hanging out together.

MILES: Hanging out together?

CARLOS: Yeah, you know, like going out with the boys, kind of thing.

MILES: With my son I wish I had had the time to have done that with him.

CARLOS: Make believe that you're doing it.

MILES: I am . . . I am, I see in you everything that I wanted to be, everything that I needed to be and everything that I would never be.

CARLOS: Oh, don't talk like that.

MILES: Why not, it's truth and the truth is an element that we should never discount, never trade in or collect green stamps on. It's free 'cause the use of it make you free or something like that.

CARLOS: I don't know, I once said the truth and I wound up in trouble. If I had lied like the rest of my pals, I would have gotten away free without my behind tan to a deep purple.

MILES: But you would have punished yourself in some other manner.

CARLOS: Oh, the old guilt trip.

MILES: Guilt is not a trip, is a solid ground that many walk on.

CARLOS: That's true, here have another drink.

MILES: Don't mind if I do.

CARLOS: Good solid ninety-proof scotch helps ease all the trips.

MILES: Until the morning light shines through your shut eyelids and wakes you up to a giant hangover.

CARLOS: Hey, is it true that the best cure for a hangover is to have a stiff drink as soon as you get up in the morning?

MILES: Before you brush your teeth.

CARLOS: Before brushing?

MILES: Before brushing.

CARLOS: Why is that?

MILES: Why is what?

CARLOS: Why is it that a good stiff drink wakes up your body after a hangover?

MILES: Because nothing else will.

CARLOS: I guess that makes sense somewhere to someone somplace.

MILES: That doesn't make no sense to me at all.

CARLOS: I know . . . should I knock? . . .

MILES: Knock . . .

CARLOS: No answer.

MILES: Maybe if you knock harder.

CARLOS: How's that?

MILES: Knock hard doesn't mean to kick down the door.

DAVID: Hey . . . hey, come on in, come on in, I'm sorry we took so long to open the door. Here, let me take your coats. Rosemarie, get the two gentlemen a drink, sit down make youself comfortable. This is a good friend of mine from New York City. He's here taking a vacation here in the great bicentennial city . . . Terry, this here is . . .

CARLOS: Carlos . . .

MILES: Miles is the name.

TERRY: Good to meet both of you. So you finished making the joint, Rosemarie?

ROSEMARIE: Yeah, here you are. . . . Would any of you like a stick of marijuana?

NICOLE: Hi, the girls are just getting the makeup together. They'll be out in a second. You like the music that's playing or would you like me to put something else on for you?

CARLOS: No, that's fine, I like the sound. Nice set you got there.

112

DAVID: Yeah, got it in the street for a price you wouldn't believe.
MILES: I can bet.
NICOLE: Here they are . . . Rita, this is Carlos.
MILES: Rita Barkley . . .
RITA: Mister.
ELAINE: Hi, everybody.
MILES: Elaine . . .
ELAINE: Dad . . . *(Lights)*

ACT II

SCENE ONE: A telephone booth.

TERRY: Yeah, yeah, I'm sure it's the right dude . . . of course, man, I
helped him out when he visited the city last year . . . sure man,
don't worry about it . . . he's out for the count . . . just make sure
that I get my bread when I get back to the city. . . . No, it's not
that I don't trust you . . . it's that I get scared of people who owe
me money they always seem to find a reason to skip out on the
payment, can you dig what I'm saying? . . . Sure . . . everything is
going to be all right . . . no, nothing is wrong . . . this dude had
this thing planned for tonight with some hicks. . . . He had a
couple of chicks for them . . . and guess what one of the chicks
turns out to be, the daughter of one of the tricks . . . yeah, young
girls, real young . . . jail bait, but they got it . . . yeah, I left as
soon as I found out what was happening, told them that I'd be
back later on tonight after everything settles down with what
happened. I wasn't about to get caught in a trap shit like that, too
much static. . . . Naw, I don't think the girl's father will call the
cops, you know kinda embarrassing for him and her, if you dig
what I mean . . . yeah, I can see what's happening from here. . . .
Man, the old man is sure doing a lot of yelling about his kid. . . .
Naw, I'll go back up after everything is over with . . . too much
static jumping off now, lights are going on everywhere in the
building. . . . How do you know I pulled the job? . . . You'll know
cause I'll be around to pick up the money, that's how. . . . I don't
collect for something I didn't pull . . . no . . . no . . . I ain't
about to keep you posted about everything that's going on . . . it
cost too much money . . . reverse the charges, you kidding . . .
no, I don't think you're going to get anything back from him. I
think he threw away the bag and kept the money . . . something
about him and his woman buying a farm . . . yeah, they wanna be
farmers, ain't that something for the book? . . . farmers. . . . No, I
don't think he kept those papers . . . maybe, but I don't think so.
. . . Why, because he's too stupid to have done that . . . no, he
ain't that smart . . . blackmail . . . are you kidding me? . . . look,
I'll be ask tonight or tomorrow morning, I got to hang up now . . .
why . . . 'cause I ain't putting no more money into this conversa-
tion, that's why . . . okay, good . . . okay . . . sure, will do, if he
got them I'll get them . . . but I don't think he does, he must have

thrown them away. I'm telling you, believe me . . . okay . . . yeah, I'll leave a mark by his body so that his people will know that he and no one else can come to the Big Apple and rip off people who are in business . . . bye . . . bye . . . I said goodbye already . . . hang up . . . what? . . . right . . . bye . . . tomorrow or tonight be on the alert. . . . Okay, will do . . . don't worry, goddamn it . . . bye . . . shit, you're one hell of a worrier, this is my last contract for you . . . no more, baby, no more hits . . . you worry too much and that's makes me leary . . . the last one and I'm serious . . . I'll take care of David Dancer for you, but he's the last one I'll do for you, no more after this, get yourself another boy . . . shit, call Detroit . . . bye . . . (Lights)

SCENE TWO: The hallway in front of David's apartment.

ROSEMARIE: Come get out of here already . . . will ya, get going, girl . . . that man is angry. He finds out that you brought his little darling up here, he's going to cause trouble for you and you don't need trouble at this stage of your life, baby . . .

NICOLE: His little darling is one of the biggest put-out artists in the whole school, next to Rita of course. . . . He's not going to do anything to me or to anyone else either.

ROSEMARIE: I know that, Baby. He's not going to do anything to you 'cause I ain't giving him the chance to do it, now get out of here, will ya, please leave this place, baby.

NICOLE: Stop pushing on me and stop calling me, baby.

ROSEMARIE: What's wrong with you, Nicole?

NICOLE: There's nothing wrong with me. What's wrong is with you pushing on me, telling me to run out on my man?

ROSEMARIE: What did you say?

NICOLE: You heard what I said . . . I ain't going nowhere. Maybe you should be running out of here but not me, I ain't going nowhere and that's that.

ROSEMARIE: Your man . . .

NICOLE: My man.

ROSEMARIE: Are you talking about David?

NICOLE: Does a bear shit in the woods?

ROSEMARIE: Are you for real?

NICOLE: Goddamn right I'm for real.

ROSEMARIE: What . . . you call David your man? . . .

NICOLE: That's right, my man . . . and I ain't running out on him either. You run if you had any feeling for that man . . . you be in there by his side not out here copping a plea. . . . He's my man, and I ain't running and leave him behind to face whatever may happen to him with that fool drunk in there. Now get out of my way and let me get back inside and stand next to my man where his woman is suppose to be.

ROSEMARIE: We'll settle this matter later.

NICOLE: There is nothing to settle.

ROSEMARIE: Later . . . we'll settle this matter later, I said.

NICOLE: And I said that there's nothing to settle.

ROSEMARIE: And I said there is . . . and we'll talk about it later, now get on out of here before I forget that you're my sister and break your little neck in three places.

NICOLE: Go on and try it, just go on and try it. You think I'm still a little baby. Take a good look at me before you raise your hands to me 'cause you better forget that I'm your sister if you so much lay a hand on me 'cause I'm sure going to forget it and do my best to kick your ass, bitch . . . now get the hell out of my way and let me back inside where I belong. You run, not me, you run, go ahead, run, leave him behind 'cause that's what he was about to do anyway with you. He was going to split on you, that's right, he had all but packed his bags on you, baby, but you didn't know what, big sister, little sister took your man, that's right, little baby innocent snotty-nose sister took your man from you and there's not a single thing you can do about it either, and you can cry and whine all you want but there's not a thing you can do about it 'cause he's my man and I'm not about to let him get into any kind of trouble without me by his side to care for him when he needs me, so get the hell out of my way this minute, hear me, get out of my way, he's mine, you blew it with him, can't you see that you're through, can you see it, are you blind to what's been going on in that house right under your nose, can't you see it? Baby, you blew the game, now it's my turn to play.

ROSEMARIE: So that's it, huh, that's the way you repay what I've gone through for you.

NICOLE: Man, stop that shit this minute 'cause you ain't done nothing for me, you did it for yourself so that you can pat yourself on the back.

ROSEMARIE: Do you believe all that shit you just said.

116

NICOLE: I don't only believe it, I can prove it, that's a fact, Baby. You always playing the big mother . . . Get out of the way.

ROSEMARIE: You really think that he's yours, don't you?

NICOLE: I know that he's mine.

ROSEMARIE: What makes you so sure, little girl?

NICOLE: 'Cause I ain't no little girl, that's what makes me so sure.

ROSEMARIE: I've been with that fool years . . . who do you think does the planning . . . who do you think does all the brainwork for the jobs that he's pulled, for the hustles that he's made, him? You really think that he does it all by himself. . . . I do it, baby, I do it. I wait for him to come out of jail . . . I wait for him to come out of wherever he is at, doing his thing, 'cause all he knows how to do is to hold a gun and point it, and that I had to teach him how to do right. . . . When he's out of bread, are you going to hit the streets to make him a dollar so that he can gamble it on a long shot . . . or spend it on some dope-head friend? . . . What do you have that makes you think that he will stick by you.? He's ready to run out on me, what makes you think that he won't do the same thing to you when he sees a piece of young flesh that turns him on? . . . You are nothing but a turn on, baby, that's all, a turn on . . . a man . . . hustlers . . . have themselves a girlfriend and they have themselves a woman . . . I'm his woman . . . you're a turn on . . . a one night stand . . . what have you got? . . . 'cause he ain't going to have much of anything once I walk out that door on him, baby. Watch him come a running . . .

NICOLE: You wanna know what I have . . . I ain't got it yet, but I will . . . I will . . . I'm going to have him . . . cause I'm gonna have his baby . . . his child.

ROSEMARIE: What did you say?

NICOLE: You heard me, you ain't got wax in your ears, right? You heard me. I'm carrying his yet-to-be born child right here, baby. You wanna feel it squirm

ROSEMARIE: You little low-life bitch . . . (Slaps her.)

NICOLE: Go on, hit me, beat me, go on, get it off your heart, baby, 'cause you're a loser, that's the only thing you're gonna leave with tonight, the satisfaction of having physically beaten me. 'Cause you lose him and you lost me and you're losing yourself.

ROSEMARIE: I'll kill him and you together. (Strangling her.)

NICOLE: Rosemarie, you're killing me, stop it . . . stop it . . .

ROSEMARIE: No, you're not to blame . . . you're just a little child, a little girl, a little baby still . . . my little baby sister . . . I didn't mean to hurt you, baby, I really didn't mean to hurt you one bit. You're not to blame, he is . . . he's a grown man who took advantage of a child infatuation, you're not to blame, he is . . . and he's going to pay . . .

NICOLE: You still believe that, don't you, that I'm a little baby, a little girl, even after I took away your man, but then he was never yours.

ROSEMARIE: No, he never was, and he'll never be yours either . . .

NICOLE: That's what you think, I'll fight for him.

ROSEMARIE: You don't have to.

NICOLE: I don't have to.

ROSEMARIE: 'Cause he's nothing to fight about.

NICOLE: He's mine, he's my man, you blew it and you're looking for an excuse to justify your loss, but there ain't none. You just couldn't handle a relationship with him like I know that I could so don't get any wild funny ideas about him or me.

ROSEMARIE: There's nothing more to be said is there?

NICOLE: Nothing.

ROSEMARIE: I'll leave . . . but let me tell you something, you or him will never make it as a team or as anything 'cause none of you have the brains to survive in this jungle of a city.

NICOLE: Run that on a news reporter or a welfare worker, not on me, don't forget we come from the same background.

ROSEMARIE: No, we don't. You never knew what it meant to be hungry or to struggle for a piece of bread. I wouldn't ever let you know that kind of life, never . . . never, but I do.

NICOLE: Well, I guess that I'm just going to have to learn.

ROSEMARIE: The pretty clothes . . .

NICOLE: I can do without them.

ROSEMARIE: Sure, you could, but can he do without his pretty clothes? You're going to get them for him, are you? . . .

NICOLE: If I have to, I will.

ROSEMARIE: Here.

NICOLE: What's that . . .

ROSEMARIE: A bank book that I've been keeping for you.

NICOLE: Put it back in your purse, I don't need it.

ROSEMARIE: That's what you think. Maybe you won't need the money, but he will. You're both going to need it, to buy a plot of land, and I know that he always wanted a fancy funeral, so make sure you get the best 'cause all I'm doing is keeping a promise to him that he would get a fancy funeral. Now it's your responsibility.

NICOLE: You're not scaring me, I'm not a child, stop acting like if I was one.

ROSEMARIE: Scared about what?

NICOLE: I know what your implying with this fancy funeral bullshit bit, and I'm not going for it. If you plan to kill us, go ahead and try.

ROSEMARIE: I did, but I couldn't do it.

NICOLE: Goodbye, big sister, get you bags and split.

ROSEMARIE: I don't want them, you keep it, keep everything . . .

NICOLE: Thank you. Don't think that I won't.

ROSEMARIE: You was welcome to my clothes, my money, my home.

NICOLE: And your man.

ROSEMARIE: And my man.

NICOLE: Goodbye . . .

ROSEMARIE: I don't hate you, but I pity you.

NICOLE: You know what you can do with your pity . . . you may not hate me but you can be sure of this, that I can't stand the sight of you and your motherly act . . . you and your pampering act . . . you and your self righteousness, sacrificing soul attitude that I had to endure each and every minute of my life with you. Now it's your turn to shed tears on an empty bed. Beat it 'cause I hate you now and always, I always hated you, you bitch . . . beat it, you heard me, I hate you, put an egg in your shoe and beat it . . . go on . . .

ROSEMARIE: I pity you 'cause you had to sneak your happiness while I worked for mine . . . and you'll never know what it means to be happy, to feel secure in that feeling because yours is a stolen love.

NICOLE: Stop singing the blues around me, either get your clothes or let the door hit you where the lord split you . . .

ROSEMARIE: Yes, I'll do that . . . a woman . . . (She laughs.)

NICOLE: Stop laughing at me, stop it I tell you, stop it, you hear me, stop laughing at me, I hate you, you dirty stinky whore, stop laughing at . . .

ROSEMARIE: I'm not laughing at you, sometimes laughter is a substitute for tears . . .

NICOLE: I told you to go sing them blues somewhere else.

ROSEMARIE: He's a sinking ship and you ain't got no life raft aboard, baby.

NICOLE: I can swim, and each night I'm going to be swimming in

his arms, while you can sing the blues . . . go get yourself drunk
. . .

ROSEMARIE: You know, that's the only sensible thing you've said today, and I think I will, bye baby, have fun.

NICOLE: Oh yes, honey, I will, the same kind that blew . . .

ROSEMARIE: Oh, by the way, I changed my mind . . . I'll take back my bank book.

NICOLE: Here, shove it.

ROSEMARIE: And tell his majesty, your man . . . that I'll send for my things in the morning . . . if he sees a morning . . .

NICOLE: They'll be ready for you . . . out in the street where they and you belong.

ROSEMARIE: You really hate me . . . pity 'cause I loved you with all my heart.

NICOLE: Peddle that somewhere else.

ROSEMARIE: Good night . . . little sister.

NICOLE: Go fuck yourself, bitch . . . that's what you're going to have to do from now on . . . do it to yourself 'cause you ain't got no man . . . I took your man . . . I took your man . . . I hate you, bitch . . . I hate you, I hope you die before morning . . . I hope you drop dead . . . (Lights.)

SCENE THREE: David Dancer's apartment.

MILES: You scum, you rat, you take young girls like this and make them defile their character. You lousy no good scum, I'm gonna kill you. (He lunges at David.)

ELAINE: Dad, don't . . .

RITA: I'm getting out of here. . . . See you later, baby. Keep my name out of this shit, you hear me, Laney . . .

ELAINE: Go on, get out of here with the rest of them.

DAVID: Mister, dig yourself, you're drunk, and I can take you out easy, now be cool before I cool you out man. Hey you, take care of this guy. Man get him off me before I hurt him.

ELAINE: Hey, come on, man, take him off before he hurts him. He's your friend so protect him, will you?

MILES: I kill you yet, mister.

DAVID: Man, you had your play, now be cool. (Punches Miles down.)

120

CARLOS: Hey, you needn't hit him that hard.

DAVID: Well, I did, now what about it? . . . Well, sucker, you let me almost break this poor jerk's jaw.

CARLOS: Look, mister, I don't want any trouble, I just came up here to have a good time. If you have something personal with him, that's your problem as well as his, not mine. So if you will get out of my way, I will open that door and leave the way I came in.

DAVID: He brought you here.

CARLOS: I know how to get back.

DAVID: And you know how to forget things too?

CARLOS: Easy . . . easy as pie . . . I forget everything like that . . .

DAVID: Make sure that you do . . .

ELAINE: What about him?

MILES: Carlos, you are deserting me, you are my friend, you are deserting me . . .

ELAINE: Some friend . . .

DAVID: Well, what are you gonna do, baby, hoof it or try to play hero. If you do, let me assure you that you are younger and not as drunk as he. My only choice will be to hurt you, and I hurt real bad, you know what I mean?

CARLOS: I'm leaving.

MILES: Coward, if you show up at the plant tomorrow, I'll make sure that you're fired . . . you punk . . . beat it.

CARLOS: Look, mister, I don't mind going off with you somewhere to have a drink and gamble and have as much fun as I could with you, because you are really a nice old man and your lies are very interesting. Hey man, I'm a realist, I don't need the job that bad and I can live without your friendship. If your friendship hinders my breathing career, can you dig it, like I play the young inno-cent type dude only because it makes you feel good. But I ain't no fool, Miles, so you handle your own personal family business and I'll handle mine. I will never ask you to break your neck for me. I never ask anyone to do that, and I never expect anyone to volunteer . . . so adiós, see you around sometime. Mr. Dancer if you would kindly let me out of your home, I will give you my word that I will not call the police because I don't wish to be involved in anything that is happening here. I'll tell the ladies outside that they can come in.

DAVID: Just hustle your ass out of here, that's all. Don't say nothing to nobody and that includes my ladies out there. I got things

121

under control, so beat it while you still have a clear path to the north . . .

CARLOS: Goodbye, Laney . . . pity, he's not a bad dude, your dad. Maybe he's a jerk with you, but not with his friends. You know I met a lot of people like that, they are lousy family members and yet they are such wonderful friends to have, always a dollar and a favor in the hand, waiting to be plucked. He like that , you know. He drinks a lot and he thinks he knows a lot, but he's just learning.

ELAINE: Bye . . .

CARLOS: Yes, I was about to leave . . . goodbye . . .

RITA: Hey, you still wanna have that good time you were looking for?

CARLOS: Sure, do you know anyone that's willing to help me find the light?

RITA: Here's a match. Come on, let's dust out of here before they start going at each other again. This ain't what I bargain for, you know . . .

CARLOS: I can imagine.

RITA: Elaine, remember, keep my name out of this.

ELAINE: Don't sweat it, baby, see you around sometime.

RITA: Call me tomorrow if you plan anything special, all right.

ELAINE: Will do, take care and have fun.

RITA: Don't I always? Like I always say make the best out of the worst . . . you still got some cash, brother?

CARLOS: Yeah, let's go. (*They exit.*)

ELAINE: You got a match?

DAVID: On the table . . .

ELAINE: Well . . . looks like the night is off, huh?

DAVID: Yeah, it looks that way.

NICOLE: Well, what are we going to do, stand here and stare at each other until the sun comes up?

ELAINE: No, I'm gonna sit down and stare for a while, you know kinda get the muscles of the brain working properly.

DAVID: Look, mister, I know that she, your daughter, I mean, I know that now, not that it would have made a bit of a difference if I had known it before she came up here, but that's the way things go . . . I mean that's life . . . man, well a part of it, the part that we are now caught up in so we have to make some kind of real-like decision on this incident. Like I don't much feel that we need to call the police into this matter, I mean, that would bring

122

on some nasty publicity from the nasty papers. You know those sensationalist rags at the news stands.

MILES: You scum.

DAVID: I wish that you stop calling me that. In fact let me tell you and take it as a warning not a threat, if you call me that one more time, I'm gonna kick your teeth in.

ELAINE: He means it, Dad.

NICOLE: Well, tell this jerk to get the hell out of here.

DAVID: Shut up, I'm running things here now . . . where's Rosemarie.

NICOLE: She left.

DAVID: Left, what ya mean she left?

NICOLE: She left, that's it. Gone for good and good riddance too. Now we have each other.

DAVID: Left for good, what ya mean she left for good? Did you have something to do with that?

NICOLE: I told her everything, and I told her that you loved me and we were going to leave together, just you and me against this world, making it.

DAVID: You told her everything . . .

NICOLE: Yes, and I told her that I was having your baby, too.

DAVID: My baby . . . you told her about having my baby, you stupid bitch, are you crazy?

NICOLE: No, I'm not crazy, maybe crazy for you, honey, but . . .

DAVID: Quit that dumb-ass rap, will ya . . . you told her about us? What makes you think that I would make it with you all the way, are you crazy? You are crazy, bitch. We'll settle this later. First, let me make sure things are going to be cool with the indignant father here.

ELAINE: Hey, Dad, he's talking about you, answer . . .

MILES: Elaine, what's gotten into you?

ELAINE: Nothing that wasn't there already. . . . Let's get this over with. Look David, I ain't pitching no bitch, and he ain't going to either 'cause he has a soft-ass job at the factory and he needs the money for his daily bottle and mom's pills are pretty low. She needs money for new prescriptions, so just make your mind at ease and let the old man out of here.

NICOLE: David, what do you mean? . . .

DAVID: Shut up, I told you once . . . you . . . I need a woman, not a little girl . . .

ELAINE: Come on, Dad, get up, sober up a little just enough to make the streets below . . .

MILES: Where did I fail?

ELAINE: On the day the doctor announced a little girl . . . get up . . .

MILES: What will your mother say?

ELAINE: Nothing. She'll take a couple of pills to hear you and then a couple more to shut you out . . . that's what you both been doing all the time, shutting me out of your life, you with your bottle and she with her pills. Well, now its out in the open at least, between you and me. She needs not to know anything and you need just to get some rest and to make yourself ready to make the liquor store in the morning, your cubbyhole is dry.

MILES: I'm getting up.

DAVID: Okay, mister, I'm sorry it had to be your daughter as much as you say you're sorry, but that's about it, just plain old verbal sorry, there's nothing to be done about it unless you make a big deal out of it, if you don't beat it.

NICOLE: Come on, get out of here already, will ya?

ELAINE: Don't rush him, he's gettin' out . . .

DAVID: If you keep your head as you been doing, life will be much easier to face from your home than it is from a hospital ward. Okay, good, that's using the old noggin, have a drink before you leave, go ahead, it's on the house . . . okay, now you can beat it.

MILES: Hold it a second, mister, I want to know how you got my little girl up here? . . . It was by force, right, you kidnapped her, didn't you say that you did that, admit it.

ELAINE: Oh stop all that bull, Dad, you know as well as I that you don't believe a word of that nonsense, so be for real.

CARLOS: I think I should be leaving, sir.

MILES: No wait . . . don't go, I may need your help with this animal.

CARLOS: My help . . .

MILES: Yes.

DAVID: Look here, mister, whatever your name is, you know that you came up here to get laid by some broad and by a young chickie as you asked for. I had no way of knowing who would be brought here. I only rent out the apartment.

MILES: Then who is the one that recruits them.

NICOLE: I do . . .

MILES: You?

NICOLE: Yes, me . . . what about it?

ELAINE: Be cool, Nicole.

NICOLE: No, you be cool . . . your old man comes here finds you making a dollar in a way that he doesn't approve and he pitches a bitch on my man, well if you ain't gonna set him straight, then I will.

MILES: Elaine.

ELAINE: He's my father, Nicole, now let me handle things here. Look Dad, I guess it's time that we stop all this crap going on between you and me. . . . First of all, you don't love or like me in the least and I can safely say that I feel the same way about you. I don't dig you at all. Maybe I'm being a little too strong on you, but that's the case. Look, I was planning on leaving you and Mom anyway to make it on my own. I don't need you anymore, and you never needed me, so I guess this takes a responsibility off your shoulders. There has never been anything for me to hold on to in that house, and I know that there never will be . . . and I don't expect . . . if after a while I stopped dreaming about it 'cause you know I always had dreams that someday you and Mom would take a few minutes off from your daily battle to offer me a sign of peace and a favor of love. I had that wonderful dream so many times that it became a re-run, stale photographs of yesterday's family album, showcasing scene in the parlor . . . life for me has begun on my terms and I am not going to give in an inch, not like you and her, you gave up yards until they became miles of living family nightmares. That's not for me. I lived with it sixteen years and I guess that there is nothing more brutal than that. Perhaps you will disown me. I really don't care, I enjoy being on my own. I've been saving every dime that I hustle to make my exit from that dreary existence that you call living. So drop it already, stop playing the concern father role. It don't fit you well and it's almost making me want to throw up all over the place, so cut it loose, will ya? . . . You had your drink, now let's go before it gets too hot up here to make it out the door . . .

DAVID: Look, mister, you came looking for a piece of pussy and you found your daughter selling hers. Maybe you should . . . you know . . . keep it in the family kinda thing.

NICOLE: Stop it, David, that's not funny.

DAVID: I'm not trying to be funny and I told you to keep your trap shut right. (*Slaps her.*)

NICOLE: I'm sorry, baby, I'll keep quiet.

DAVID: That goes to show you that Humphrey Bogart was right. I never met a woman who didn't understand a good slap in the mouth . . .

ELAINE: Come on, Dad, this scene ain't your scene.

125

DAVID: Elaine, this scene ain't a lot of people's scene, but it's a scene that's for real, that goes on everyday in one of the cubby holes that fill the streets of this city and we, you, as well as your father and hundreds like him, close your ears to the struggle to survive and everything that a ghetto dweller finds that makes him a dollar without giving it to the government, like the politician never does, but it a part of a hustle, baby. If you're planning on leaving the womb, then make sure that your stomach can stand the food that you must serve yourself in order to live.

ELAINE: I can handle it.

DAVID: See you around surviving.

ELAINE: I hope so.

MILES: I'm a loser . . . a loser . . . oh god.

ELAINE: Come on Dad, don't cry . . . not everyone is a winner.

DAVID: Hey, mister, you know some people say that there's nothing wrong with being on the losing team and, you know that's a whole lot of bullshit . . . in my world, first is first and second is nobody and third is obsolete . . . get out of here, you loser. (Miles and Elaine exit.)

ELAINE: Throw me my cigarettes . . . thanks, loser . . .

DAVID: I'm a winner . . . I was born to win. . . . Look at this mess . . . come on, get your ass up and get out of here.

NICOLE: Get out?

DAVID: Yeah, you heard me, get the hell out.

NICOLE: But what about us?

DAVID: Us?

NICOLE: Yes, us goddamn it, us, me and you.

DAVID: There is no us, there's only a you and there's only a me, and that's the way I want to keep it . . .

NICOLE: But . . .

DAVID: No buts, just get out.

NICOLE: I need you.

DAVID: I don't need you.

NICOLE: I don't have Rosemarie anymore.

DAVID: Thanks to you, I don't have her either . . . she'll probably send for her things in the morning and she's the type of woman that once she makes her mind to leave, she's leaving. Goddamn it, that was the best woman that I ever had and I blew it. Why didn't you just let things ride? . . . everything was going along so nicely, but you had to be greedy, shit . . .

NICOLE: Baby, I only wanted to be with you.

DAVID: Well, you were with me, wasn't you . . . didn't we spend time together? What more did you want, a fucking marriage? I bet that's it . . . man, what a fool I was . . .

NICOLE: You got me, baby, you got me . . . I'll hustle the streets for you . . . I'll make money for both of us . . .

DAVID: You're just a little fucking squirt . . . you ain't got the class nor the stamina to keep it up in this hustle like your sister. She's a woman, I need me a woman, not a sixteen-year-old school twenty-five cent piece of pussy . . . I need a woman, now beat it. I need you like I need a policeman knocking on my door. . . . Come on, get out . . . I got to get some rest and go out to find me a woman . . . twenty dollars, that's all the money you got, huh? . . . Here's your bag, get out cause you ain't my bag . . . (*He grabs her by the arm and physically throws her out of the apartment. She cursing and pleading with him. He begins to clean up his place. Doorbell.*) Yeah, who is it? . . . who . . . oh, yeah man, come on in come on in. . . . Hey man, excuse the place but I had quite a busy night as you well know . . . real hassle with all that went on here . . . a real hassle you'd never believe the shit that jumped off in here tonight, man . . . you tipped off in a hurry, man in a flash like lightening hurry . . . I guess I can nickname you superman and I'd be close right.

TERRY: No, I have no nicknames . . . I really don't need any visitors bearing bad breath on your door while I'm here visiting you, can you dig it man.

DAVID: Sure . . . sure, I was just joking . . . you know, busting your balls . . . man, everything went wrong tonight . . . nothing stood on the road tonight . . . my life might be well described as a slippery highway. . . . There I am, an invited trick and a whore staring at each other and they turn out to be family . . . wow, what a trip, man, what a trip . . . god I'm lucky that the dude was a cold loser hooked on the juice and not one of the gamblers of the streets, elsewise I'd be in a world of trouble. . . . I might as well write the day off to experience, that always works. . . . The little chick you met with the big ass, Rosemarie's little sister, she goes off and tells Rosemarie, my woman?, that she's been laying in bed with me. . . . Rosemarie walks out on me after that . . . and she's the type of broad that does not make a comeback after she out of the stage . . . hope she ain't never coming into my bed again, not on this side of hell . . . you know man, she was one helluva woman, man, couldn't do better with a dog . . . so what ya gonna do man . . . you could crash here until you don't need the place anymore. Me, I got to get me a nice hot bath and a . . . a . . . a . . . hell, I don't know what else I need to make me feel better, but a hot hot bath will do for openers . . . man, let me tell you I must have woke up on the wrong side of the bed this morning 'cause nothing really has gone right at all . . . nothing at all, that's a bitch . . . everybody gone . . . all the smoke smoked up, the liquor gone . . . nothing left but some warm beer. That's what I got to leave behind in my will, my great estate, a pack of warm beer . . . and a half of pack of stale cigarettes . . . had to throw that little bitch out, a girl like that is a one-way ticket to prison or to an early grave. . . . Yep, she's the type that'll cause a man a lot of unnecessary pain and discomfort . . . that's why I don't deal with young meat for any length of time, can't handle it . . . and it ain't worth the risk . . . you wanna take a bath while I finish, you're welcome . . . can you hear me? . . . today has been a day that I won't want somebody to recite over my coffin during the text of my eulogy . . . hell no, you know what, Terry . . . I guess today just ain't my day . . . (*Terry has during the course of David's speech prepared his gun with a silencer and walks into the bathroom.*)

TERRY: I guess not . . . (*Curtain.*)